Yale Series in Economic History

Men and Wealth
in the United States
1850-1870

LEE SOLTOW

New Haven and London
Yale University Press
1975

Library of Congress catalog card number: 74–29738
International standard book number: 0–300–01814–2

Set in IBM Baskerville type.
Printed in the United States of America by
The Murray Printing Company, Forge Village, Mass.

Published in Great Britain, Europe, and Africa by
Yale University Press, Ltd., London.
Distributed in Latin America by Kaiman & Polon,
Inc., New York City; in Australasia and Southeast
Asia by John Wiley & Sons Australasia Pty. Ltd.,
Sydney; in India by UBS Publishers' Distributors Pvt.,
Ltd., Delhi; in Japan by John Weatherhill, Inc., Tokyo.

Contents

Tables and Charts

Appendix Tables

Charts

Foreword

Lee Soltow's book contains something for almost—though
not quite—everyone. For the radical and cynic, it lays bare
a shocking picture of inequality. It shows the proportion of
Americans in the mid-nineteenth century who held no wealth
at all (about three-eighths). It reveals how much poorer the
foreign born were than native Yankees, city dwellers than
farmers, blacks than whites. Fifty-nine percent of the white
male population in 1850 had no landed wealth; only about
23 percent had individual holdings of at least $1,000. This
23 percent, in fact, owned 92 percent of the total value of
real estate in the country.

So much, one might say, for the American dream. But was
that the dream? The conservative views America as the land,
not of equal wealth, but of equal opportunity; there is much
in Soltow's meticulous examination of the statistical evidence
from the mid-nineteenth-century census returns to warm the
conservative's heart. Comparing per capita wealth held by
men in the different age classes in 1860 Soltow finds that the
distribution follows a curve, rising to age 60, then falling off.
The curve for foreign-born males parallels at a lower level that
for the native population. It seems a fair assumption that this
cross section of age classes does in fact embalm the history of
individuals as they moved through the central decades of the
nineteenth century. This is particularly plausible since the
distributions and differentials remain reasonably stable over
the three census years that Soltow studies. If so, then a young
man in 1860 might expect rising wealth as he moved through
life, and a young immigrant might expect not only his own
lot to improve, but also that of his native-born children, who
would begin life at a higher wealth level than he had enjoyed.

Of course not all readers have a political axe to grind.
Scholars who have methodologies instead of blood in their

veins will also meet here with their rewards. The historian, suspicious as he may be of econometrics, will find this study surely a most acceptable example of "quantification." It puts solid flesh on the American dream, weighs it in the balance of the census returns and shows precisely, for all the regions and several important groups of the population, its true anatomy. Soltow's exposition is difficult, but his statistical methods are not really very recondite and his conclusions, based on average and distributions, are derived from that most authentic and respected of historical sources: what people said about themselves at the time. The development economist too will be intrigued by yet another example of the pervasiveness of wealth inequality in human societies and by the stability of the distributions over time. Much interesting work has been begun, both by economic theorists and by students of economic development, into income and wealth distribution. Soltow's study is one of the most solid, best documented, and ingeniously worked out of any that has yet appeared.

Only one sort of reader will not find much for him in this book: the reader who wants research thoroughly predigested before it is put on the table. Those who have read Soltow's earlier studies know the problem. Of his study on Wisconsin, I wrote that, as Huck Finn said of the Bible, it was "good readin' but tough." The present book is even better "readin'"; the scope is a whole nation in all its parts, the coverage is three most fateful decades of American history throughout the major divisions of the country; the inclusion of the Southern states before and after the elimination of slaves as a form of wealth make this far richer and more rewarding than the Wisconsin study. But the exposition is correspondingly even more intricate. Soltow is one of those ineradicably honest research scholars who are far more interested in their data than in their readers and seem to take an almost perverse delight in burying sensational conclusions in a jungle of technique and qualification. Some minds find this abhorrent; but some find it challenging, and it is for the latter that this book is intended. Those wh do not like Soltow's puzzles can still profit from the discussion at many points and particularly from the clear and modestly stated conclusions in the final chapter. Soon—almost too soon—what is said there will become part of the stock in trade of history texts, enlarged upon, generalized about, and twisted to fit one argument or another. Soltow presents here the plain, unvarnished, statistical truth about American wealth distribution in the mid-nineteenth century. Let others, more fanciful or more journalistic, make of it what they will.

William N. Parker
Yale University

Preface

The dream of a quantitative economist might be to cover all time and space in considering every individual who has ever lived. Each individual might have been asked a question concerning the value of his economic well-being at various points of time throughout his life. The data would be used to study the economic progress of different subsets of individuals and the distribution of resources among these and larger subcultures.

A unique beginning was made in the United States in the remarkably early census year of 1850. Each individual was asked not only his residence, age, occupation, nativity, and color. He was also asked to quantify his economic well-being by stating the value of real estate that he owned. Furthermore, the manuscripts of this census are readily available on microfilm. Part of this book is devoted to a report of a probability sample of individuals drawn from this census.

This was more than a census of agriculture; in fact, three-eighths of the aggregate value of real estate was held by nonfarmers. It was more than a tax roll of the rich; many had real estate of less than $500 in value. We are not limited to drawing Pareto curves of the rich; the distribution in one sense forms a beautiful logarithmic normal curve. This was more than a census of homogeneous peoples; one-ninth of aggregate estate was held by foreign born. It was a census of more than the real estate of a county, state, or region: of aggregate estate, three-tenths was held by men living in slave states, five-tenths by men living in the Northeast, and two-tenths by those living in the new Northwest area west of Pennsylvania. It was a census of more than the old: one-tenth of real estate was held by those under 30 years of age.

A study of the 1850 census question is a quantification of the economic aspects of the existing social issues of America: the westward movement, the power of the South, urbanization, and assimilation of foreign-born groups. It can even be a quantification of the economic power involved in the generation gap. As but one example of these problems, consider the cross classification of residence and birth. What was the average estate of those born in the Northeast living in the Northeast compared to those born in the Northeast but living in the Northwest? Did the fittest remain or move to the frontier? An even more important classification pertains to age groups. The average real estate of men of age 50-59 can be compared to that of men of 20-29. The former group has participated in economic growth for a generation longer than the latter. It was of age 20-29 in 1820. Thus, age is a proxy for time and we can begin to explore ramifications of growth over time by looking at the real estate–age patterns in the given year 1850.

The question of economic well-being was not only continued in 1860; it was also expanded to include the value of the personal estate of the individual. This was all the more remarkable because personal estate of freemen in the South included the value of slaves. And this was but six months before the beginning of the Civil War. I report here the results of a probability sample of the 1860 census. One of the many ways in which I will express the economic power of whites in the South is in the finding that three-sevenths of total U.S. aggregate market wealth of individual freemen was held in the South.

One now can compare real estate holdings over time so that an age and time dimension can be obtained: those 40-49 in 1850 were 50-59 in 1860. It is possible to build a model encompassing age and time. We should also consider the vector of space, since different areas of the country developed at different rates of growth. The main object is to see how economic growth was ramified in the lives of individuals as they grew 10 years older in age and in time.

Finally, quantitative questions on real estate and personal estate were asked again in 1870. I report the results of a probability sample of these census manuscripts. The most dramatic change in the economic well-being of people in the country should be embedded in the 1860-70 census manuscripts. If the inequality of ownership of wealth had ever changed radically, it would have been in this decade. If one had the choice of only two census years in the history of the United States from which to study a substantial and permanent shift, he would have to choose this period. Ironically, the census volumes for 1930 and 1940 or 1940 and 1950 do not chronicle statistically the change in well-being of individuals as thoroughly as do our figures for 1860-70. The 1870 census officials were the last to ask the economic question of all men in various occupations until census officials introduced the limited question on wages and salaries in the 1940 census.

This volume is a study of these precious 1850, 1860, and 1870 records of man's achievement. These records help us understand not only the depressing aspects of the inequality of man but also the basis of his hope for economic betterment and his acceptance of a system of rugged capitalism and individualism, which stemmed from his own past economic accumulation of wealth and that of others, particularly elders, whom he knew.

I already have had the benefit of making an extensive study, *Patterns of Wealthholding in Wisconsin Since 1850,* prior to undertaking this report for the entire country. The two works are complementary in many ways. The earlier one is an in-depth analysis of the economic transformation of a frontier state. The present book is more authoritative in the sense that it covers all areas of the United States and emphasizes the major problem of slavery. I wistfully must admit, however, that the Wisconsin study was tied much more closely and intimately to people as individuals.

The study that has resulted in the book at hand was supported largely by grants from the National Science Foundation. Strong support was also given by Ohio University in the form of a reduced teaching schedule. I particularly wish to thank an unknown reader of the Wisconsin work for helping me understand which procedures and themes were of merit and which were not. I thank the administration, the faculty, and students of my university for giving me the time necessary to work on this topic. However, the conclusions, opinions, and other statements in this book are mine and not necessarily those of any of the persons or groups mentioned above.

Introduction to the Census Manuscripts

The United States censuses for 1850, 1860, and 1870 asked
each person to state how much he was worth. The instruc-
tions to the enumerators in 1860 read as follows:

> *Value of Real Estate.* Under heading 8, insert the value
> of real estate owned by each individual enumerated.
> You are to obtain this information by personal inquiry
> of each head of a family, and are to insert the amount
> in dollars, be the estate located where it may. You are
> not to consider any question of lien or encumbrance; it
> is simply your duty to enter the value as given by the
> respondent.
>
> *Value of Personal Estate.* Under heading 9, insert (in
> dollars) the value of personal property or estate. Here
> you are to include the value of all the property, posses-
> sions, or wealth of each individual which is not embraced
> in the column previous, consist of what it may; the value
> of bonds, mortgages, notes, slaves, live stock, plate, jewels,
> or furniture; in fine, the value of whatever constitutes the
> personal wealth of individuals. Exact accuracy may not
> be arrived at, but all persons should be encouraged to
> give a near and prompt estimate for your information.
> Should any respondent manifest hesitation or unwilling-
> ness to make a free reply on this or any other subject,
> you will direct attention to Nos. 6 and 13 of your gen-
> eral instructions and the 15th section of the law.

The value of each man's real estate was asked for in all three
censuses; in 1860 and 1870 the value of his personal property
was also required.

If we collate these answers with answers to the other questions in the censuses on age, sex, color, nativity, occupation,
and place of residence, we can uncover facts about the wealth

accumulation by young and old, native and foreign born,
farmers and city dwellers, in all the areas of the United
States.[1] The manuscripts of these censuses are also the first
to give details about the individual members of families.
Our problem is to extract from them as much important
information as we can about various socioeconomic groups
in the United States.

A Glimpse at the Manuscripts

Let us select the page of the census taker's manuscripts for
1860 for a certain street in Springfield, Illinois. We find the
following information from lines 17 to 22 of page 740 of
the bound manuscripts:

					Value of estate owned		
					---	---	---
				Occu-	Real	Personal	
Line	*Name*	*Age*	*Sex*	*pation*	*estate*	*estate*	*Birth*
17	Abraham Lincoln	51	m	Lawyer	$5,000	$12,000	Kentucky
18	Mary "	35	f				"
19	Robt. "	16	m				Illinois
20	Willie "	9	m				"
21	Thomas "	7	m				"
22	M. Johnson	18	f	Servant			"

The household head listed just before this entry was a 50-
year-old man born in Ireland who reported $30,300 in
wealth. The household head listed immediately below
Lincoln was a 38-year-old individual born in Maryland and
having $300 in wealth. One could find in Springfield several
men with estates of over $100,000 within a few pages of
the Lincoln entry and two older bankers, born in the East,
with estates of more than $500,000. There would then ap-
pear more and more entries for men with no wealth, and
overall the evidence is of great unevenness of wealth distribution in Springfield. Lincoln's total estate of $17,000 (about
$68,000 in 1970 prices) meant that he was a relatively rich

man. The average wealth for free adult males in the United
States was about $2,500.

One cannot help but be impressed by the affluence of the
very rich men of Springfield who listed coachmen, gardeners,
and as many as three servants as part of their households.
On the other hand many listings give $0 for both real estate
and personal estate. The foreign born and the young appear
to have had little or no wealth. Was Springfield, then, a city
with a few affluent men and an upper class (lawyers, doctors,
merchants, and officials) of perhaps fewer than 5 percent of
its inhabitants? The lower class is clearly demarcated as the
group with no wealth; those listing occupation as laborer,
day laborer, or none at all must have formed a bottom layer.
Springfield may very well have been a city with the economic
classes, if not the social classes, of any modern city.[2] It was
a city more closely tied to agriculture than to manufacturing,
with affluent farmers, farmers, and farm laborers in its out-
skirts.

But Springfield was not Chicago or Boston or Natchez. The
manuscript census volume of Chicago lists

			Occu-	*Value of estate owned*		
				Real	Personal	
Name	Age	Sex	pation	estate	estate	Birth
William Ogden	55	m	Lawyer	$1,500,000	$1,000,000	New York
Cyrus McCormick	50	m	Reaper factory	278,000	1,750,000	Virginia

However, one would find dozens and dozens of pages of
names listing no wealth. The pauper and his wife might be
Irish born and "unable to read and write." Still, an illiterate
man might be a carpenter with $1,000 in wealth. A leap to
the pages for Natchez, Mississippi, in 1860 would reveal
estates above $100,000 listed much more frequently than in
Springfield, Illinois. Whereas much the greater proportion
of wealth was held in the form of real estate in the North,
the reverse was true in the South. The simple fact was that

personal estate in the South included the value of slaves. A quick check of the 1870 volume for Natchez would demonstrate that affluence had vanished.

These are but glimpses of selected areas of America in the middle of the nineteenth century. Each area is worth a detailed study with respect to its socioeconomic classes as determined by age, occupation, color, birth, and wealth. The distribution of wealth has implications for income distribution, consumption, and savings patterns. We could study each area for the periods 1850 to 1860 to 1870 for the ramifications of economic growth on the rise and decline of different socioeconomic groups. The strength of a study of a local area is that it may be tied closely to details of individuals and local events; the weakness is that the area may be unique in its characteristics and thus unsuitable as a sample of the United States or of any large region—the South, the North, or the Northwest.

We wish to have valid results for the country as a whole and its major areas. To do this, we must draw from all areas a random sample of measurable characteristics for all people (age, nativity, color) related to their wealth. Only then can an authoritative economic study of wealth, income, consumption, and saving be made. A random sample depersonalizes the data and loses details of individuals and local issues. But the job must be done to acquire reliable knowledge of some characteristics of all the rich and poor in America in the mid-nineteenth century.

The Spin Samples from the Manuscripts

To ensure a random selection of a line (or individual) from the pages of the census manuscripts, I developed a spin procedure for a microfilm roll on a microfilm reader. In taking the sample for 1860, for example, I designated a given spot on the screen of the microfilm reader. The first film was attached and half-turns of the feeder arm were made until a completed entry line of the manuscript fell on the spot. The entry was chosen for the sample if it was a male 20 years old or older. I continued half-turns to the end of the film and examined nonempty lefthand entries if they fell on the spot. At this point the procedure was reversed: the film was fed through the machine backward, and righthand pages were considered. Succeeding films were fed through the machine, alternating lefthand–forward and righthand–backward directions with righthand–forward and lefthand–backward directions. I used similar procedures for the microfilms for 1850 and 1870. Those persons with wealth of $100,000 or more were sampled 40 times more heavily in 1860 and 10 times more heavily in 1850 than those under $100,000. A sample in a given year will be called a spin sample. Spin samples taken of the free adult male populations in the three censuses gave sample sizes of 10,393 in 1850, 13,696 in 1860, and 9,823 in 1870.

Validity of the Spin Samples

The census officials published only one compilation pertaining to our wealth data; this 1860 table listed the aggregate value of real and personal estate.[3] The mean wealth of an adult male fell between $2,510 and $2,540, well within the $90 standard error of the mean of the spin sample. Real estate was .577 for the published table and .573 for the spin sample. The samples have almost perfect proportional representation from each state and territory in the United States. This occurs because sample items were chosen at fairly regular intervals per running foot of the microfilm manuscript lists of names arranged by areas within counties. All published census tables for adult males 20 and older in the United States are in excellent accord with the spin sample results. Age representation is good even for the age groups 60-69 and 70-99. The proportion of nonwhite in 1870 was .110 in the population and .112 in the sample. The number of

farmers in the sample with real estate is quite consistent
with the number reported in census tables. Published census
figures for all persons, classified by region or country of
birth, seem to be consistent with those adult males in the
spin samples.

The wealth averages for the spin samples in the years
1850-70 are also generally in line with estimates, interpolations, and extrapolations of estimates made by various
authorities on wealth distribution. Growth rates are similar
to those found for gross national product per worker by
Kuznets and commodity output per worker by Gallman.[4]
Particularly striking are the similarities between Gallman's
figures and our spin-sample results for the northern states.
Some aggregates obtained from county assessors and adjusted to "true" values by assessors and others for the years
1850, 1860, and 1870 are also fairly consistent with spin-
sample results. There is an indication that individuals in
1870 may have understated their wealth or did not adjust
to price changes, but in general we find exceedingly consistent relationships of variables in the 1850, 1860, and
1870 figures. Other aspects of the consistency of the data
have been discussed by the author in a companion volume
entitled *Patterns of Wealthholding in Wisconsin Since 1850.*
Results to be presented here are consistent with the complete census of wealth of Australia in 1915 and with U.S.
censuses of slave owners from 1790 on.[5] They are also consistent with results of samples drawn by Gallman.[6]

Plan of the Study

The subject of this book is the economic well-being of men
in the United States in the two decades following 1850.
But in many ways it is also a book that concerns the first
half of the nineteenth century because we are dealing with
men of differing socioeconomic backgrounds, some of
whom were born in the eighteenth century. The index of

well-being for each man is his wealth, which is a historical
concept because it is a record of his past accumulation. The
essence of wealth is past saving, inheritance, and capital
gains. My purpose is to describe the extent of accumulation
for various groups in society while at the same time convey-
ing the magnitude of wealth inequality within groups. I will
relate the findings for midcentury to wealth studies that
have been conducted from that time to the present.

Chapter 1 classifies the populations of men in 1850, 1860,
and 1870 by whether or not they were young or old, native
born or foreign born, farmers or nonfarmers. The greater
relative number of young in cities and old in rural areas will
be quantified. It is possible to trace time trends in urbanization and immigration by noting age characteristics of men
in a given year such as 1850 or 1860. A study of the extent
to which populations of men shared in the American dream
is the subject of chapter 2. The qualitative variable considered is whether or not an individual owned a house or land
or some other equivalent minimum level of wealth. I will
offer various characteristics of the poor without property.

Chapters 3 and 4 consider the dollar amounts of wealth
held by all men and by various groups in covering the gamut
from have-nots through various levels of wealthholding
among the haves to those who were very rich men. More
specifically, chapter 3 deals with the arithmetic averages of
wealth distribution and chapter 4 describes the relative
dispersion or inequality of these distributions. One learns
in chapter 3 about changes in average real estate from 1850
to 1860 and the changes in mean total estate from 1860 to
1870 for all men and for various socioeconomic groups. I
will particularly note improvements for age cohorts of men
as they grew older. Chapter 4 is in a sense an extension of
chapter 3 since we study the wealth averages of the poor,
those of middle wealth, and the rich in ascertaining how inequality of wealth changed at midcentury. Inequality in
1850 and 1860 is compared with levels of earlier times;

levels in 1870 are compared with estimates of inequality
since that time.

Chapter 5 is concerned with the inequality of farmland
and slaveholdings to the extent that they help explain the
inequality of dollar estates in the farm sector. Land distributions are available since 1850 and slave distributions are
extant for 1790 to 1860. They are tied to our estate statistics at midcentury to provide ideas about maldistribution
from 1790 to the present. Knowledge of slave frequency
tables in 1860 is fundamental to understanding what hap-
pened to southern estate distribution during the Civil War
decade.

Chapter 6 provides a special analysis of wealth characteristics of persons born in several different foreign countries
and in various states and regions of the United States. I
make a study of counties in the United States of low and
high wealth with respect to a wide spectrum of demographic
variables. The final chapter of the book provides a succinct
general summary of the conclusions offered at the end of
each chapter. It is from this information that we uncover
the hierarchy of ownership in this country before and after
the Civil War and the ways in which the power of wealth of
elite groups changed. The strong level of inequality before
and after the war must be understood in terms of the rapid
advance in economic accumulation experienced by the
majority of men during their productive years.

1. Age Composition and Population Growth

It is fruitful to begin our study by considering only the sizes of the various populations classified by age, nativity, and occupation. How youthful was the labor force? How were the immigration movement and rural–urban movements manifested in classifications by age groups at different points in time? We wish to provide a proper setting for the dynamic changes that occurred in the middle of the nineteenth century. This chapter differs from those that follow because it considers only sizes of populations, not amounts of wealth.

The spin samples yield two classifications of population data for the United States not elsewhere available. They are age-specific populations classified by nativity for 1850 and 1860 and age-specific populations classified by occupation for 1850-60-70. Figures for native-born age groups in 1850 reflect population growth in the country prior to 1850. This material helps us introduce the idea that *age* groups in the middle of the century are a very interesting and realistic proxy for *history* in the first half of the nineteenth century. Estimates of the extraordinary deaths of native born from 1860 to 1870 also can be determined. Occupation classifications by age group indicate the long-run trend toward urbanization.

The Age Composition of the Free Adult Male Population

The free adult male population of the United States in 1850 was youthful by almost any standard. Its average age was 37 compared to an average of 44 in 1970. Thirty-eight percent lay between the ages 20 and 29 compared to 26 percent in that age group today. Now the rate of growth of a population over time is intimately related to its age distribution at any

point in time. Consider the number of persons in each of
the six age classes in 1850 as given in table 1.1 and plotted
in chart 1.1.

Table 1.1. Distribution of Adult Males among Age Classes

Population		*Age class*					
		20-29	30-39	40-49	50-59	60-69	70 *and up*
U.S. whites	1860	.361	.270	.177	.107	.058	.028
Great Britain	1861	.305	.238	.191	.132	.085	.048
Ireland	1861	.32	.20	.17	.16	.09	.05
Me., N.H., Vt.,	1860	.308	.222	.182	.139	.091	.058
Ia., Ill., Ind.	1860	.387	.277	.168	.103	.048	.018
U.S. whites	1830	.406	.251	.156	.097	.057	.032
U.S. total population	1900	.322	.254	.188	.124	.072	.041
U.S. total population	1970	.257	.183	.193	.166	.116	.086

Sources: Historical Statistics of the United States, series A 51-58,
71-85, various censuses of the United States, and U.S. Bureau of the
Census, "Summary of Demographic Projections," series P-25, no. 388,
Mar. 14, 1968; B. R. Mitchell, *Abstract of British Historical Statistics,*
pp. 12-14 (stated Irish class limits necessitated interpolation).

Chart 1.1 shows that the age profile (the relative numbers
in each age group) falls off at a slightly increasing rate,
particularly after age 50 for all the groups. If there had been
no immigration into the United States between 1780 and
1850 and if all the persons born in that period had lived
until 1850, this profile would perfectly reflect the births
over the first 50 of these 70 years. The problem of immigration can be disposed of by examining the age profile of
the native-born population alone (1850 NB in chart 1.1).
The incidence of death can be estimated, though not perfectly, by use of the age-specific death rates available in
data for Massachusetts and for England and Wales in this
period.[1]

Thus a line fitted to the log data for native born from age

Chart 1.1. Number of Adult Males at Each Year of Age in the United States, 1850, 1860, and 1870

Number per
year of age
(thousands;
log scale)

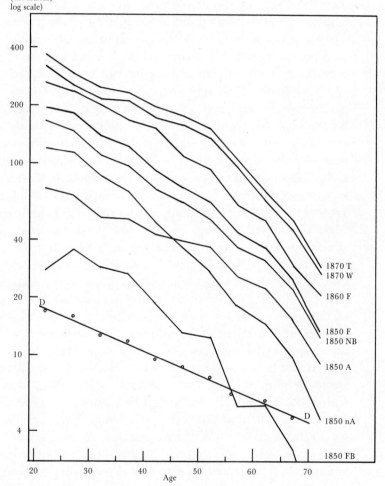

Sources: Spin samples and *Historical Statistics,* series A 71-85, B 169-175. The death inflator is a chained Massachusetts index for 1865.

Note: Line D shows the relative 1850 native-born population by age group, making an allowance for estimated deaths occurring in each age cohort before 1850 (see text).

Symbols: T total population, F free population, W white population, NB native born, A farmers, nW nonwhite population, FB foreign born, nA nonfarmers.

20 to 69[2] yields an apparent growth rate of .045, or 4.5 percent per annum, but this is an overstatement of true growth over time by the deaths that this population had incurred. Eighteen sixty-five death-rate figures for Massachusetts for ages 20-69 indicate a reasonably straight line when cast in the form of the reciprocal of the probability of living after age 20. The slope of the line indicates an average death adjustment of 1.6 percent for each year of age. This death adjustment applied to the 4.5 percent apparent growth rate yields an estimated rate of 2.9 percent. We shall have occasion to use .029 or .030 as the growth rate of the native-born population and .035 as the growth rate of the total population. The number of all white adult males from each of the six censuses from 1800 to 1850 has an exponential trend averaging 3.5 percent a year.[3] Table 1.1 gives comparative age composition figures for the British Isles. The United States as a whole clearly had a younger adult population than that of Britain or Ireland, but the pattern in upper New England is already close to the British one, in strong contrast to that in Iowa, Illinois, and Indiana in 1860. The age composition of the older states, like that of European countries, may be characterized as settled with relative outmigration; in the western region two of every three adult males were not yet 40. The population in the United States as a whole in 1830 was similar to that of the western region in 1860. The population-age gradient of the United States gradually fell until 1900, when it reached the European gradient of 1860. Note the United States gradient for 1970, when youth is relatively scarce. Clearly, settlement is strongly associated with youth. This fact, in turn, will be found to contribute strongly to inequality in wealthholding in newly settled regions.

Nativity and Age

The number of foreign born in the 1850 census increased

between ages 20 and 27 and then decreased exponentially
after age 30. Of course these age groups had experienced
not only deaths but also new arrivals in their midst every
year as they had grown older. However, if we assume that
the average age of arriving immigrants did not change over
time, the death-inflated population–age pattern in 1850
would reflect the long-run time trend of immigration.

The apparent growth rate AGR_N was greater for foreign
born than for native born. For the data from age 25 to 69,
the death-inflated equation gives a rate of .062- .016 ~
.045. This far exceeds the apparent rate for any of the foreign countries given in table 1.1. The relatively small number of foreign born of old age shown in chart 1.1 indicates
that there were few foreign-born males prior to 1820. The
figures of $AGR_{N,1850,NB}$ and $AGR_{N,1850,FB}$ presage
the direction but not the extent of the spin-sample findings,
which show that the proportion of foreign born among
adult white males increased from .179 in 1850 to .258 in
1860 and .278 in 1870. The censuses of 1840 and earlier
did not include nativity questions.

We wish to know the American experience in wealth
accumulation of foreign born, not their European experience.
Two missing facts in the statistics are the number of years a
foreign-born male has lived in the United States and the
wealth he brought in with him. The comparison of wealth
averages of those 25-29 and 55-59 may not reflect 30 years'
difference in American experience. Fresh arrivals each year
can depress the wealth average of each group. Fortunately,
the population–age pattern of arrivals shows the preponder-
ance of individuals to be very young. The figures for arrivals
of adult males are available for 1845, 1847, and 1852. Totals
for the three years combined, expressed as a proportion of
all foreign born in the United States in 1850, were .56 for
those 20-29, .28 for those 30-39, and .15 for those 40 and
older. It is conceivable that in 1850 the period of residence
in the United States of those 55-59 was not more than 20

years. The length of experience in this country must have
increased substantially from 1860 to 1870; the gains in
average wealth of the foreign-born population will reflect
this fact.

Occupation of the Population

The most intriguing population–age patterns are those for
farmers and nonfarmers. Chart 1.1 shows that these two
patterns for 1850 are essentially straight exponential lines
crossing between ages 40 and 49. The line for nonfarmers
is substantially steeper, indicating a greater apparent growth
rate.

There is a deficiency in the 1850 classification because
farm laborers generally were not included as farmers. The
1860 figures do include farm laborers and we look for long-
run trends by considering farmers and nonfarmers in that
year. Each forms an excellent death-inflated exponential
configuration from age 20 to 69 with the two lines inter-
secting at about age 37, the arithmetic mean of age. (Farmer
and nonfarmer lines for each nativity class are given in
chart 1.2.) There is evidence that nonfarm population was
increasing each year at a rate (4.4 percent) twice that of the
farm population. The implication of the 1860 equations is
that the proportion of farmers in the total population
would have fallen from .495 to .463 in a decade. The actual
proportion given in the census for adult males was .495 in
1860 and .462 in 1870. The straight-line equations for
farmers and total population intersect at an age of 112
years. The resultant implication that all 20 year olds were
farmers about a century before 1860 is very roughly consistent with history. The total number of workers, presumably from 10 years of age and for both sexes, is reported
for 1820 to 1860 in *Historical Statistics*.[4] The average
annual percentage of change was 2.8 for farmers and 4.3
for nonfarmers. These figures contrast with our spin-sample

Chart 1.2. Death-Inflated Lines of Apparent Population Growth for Adult Males in 1860 for Farmers, Nonfarmers, Native Born, and Foreign Born for Selected Age Groups

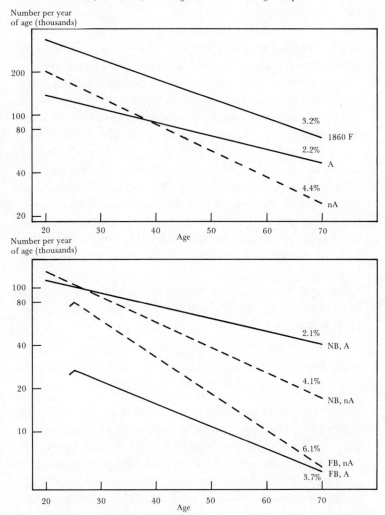

Source: See chart 1.1.

Note: Straight lines have been fitted for ages 20-69 for free and native born and for 25-69 for foreign born.

data for 1860, which show apparent rates of 2.2 and 4.4 percent for ages 20-69.

Occupation–Nativity Groups

It is interesting to study apparent growth rates of nativity groups when they are further classified by farmer-non-farmer groups. I will use the lines presented in chart 1.2 to describe the situation in 1860. Among native born the number of farmers was substantially greater than that of non-farmers except at the younger age level. The ratio of the two was nearly 1/1 at age 20 and 2.5/1 at age 70. Here is a strong manifestation of this pervasive trend prior to the Civil War. Among foreign born the number of nonfarmers was substantially greater than that of nonfarmers among the young but the same among old. This time the ratio is roughly 2.5/1 among the young and 1/1 among the old. Four of every 10 of age 30-35 in urban (nonfarm) areas were foreign born.

The proportion of farmers was much higher among native born than among the foreign born, as the accompanying table shows.

	1860	1870
NB	.556	.537
FB	.318	.241

The 1870 figures could be anticipated from the 1860 configurations. The apparent growth rates of 1860, shown in the top and bottom portions of chart 1.2, have been adjusted for deaths and are for ages 20-69 for native born and 25-69 for foreign born. The apparent population growth rates among native born in 1860 of .021 for farmers and .041 for nonfarmers are calculated to give a proportion of .538 farmers in 1870. Foreign-born rates of .037 and .061 for these two groups lead to a .270 proportion of farmers among the foreign born in 1870. The fundamental point of all these calculations is that the rural–urban movement was governed by long-run, slowly changing forces. The direction and extent of the movement by 1870 can be predicted from the pattern in 1860.

The scheme of apparent growth breaks down after the Civil War. It is difficult to establish rates for 1870 because of the effect of war deaths on the age group 24-44 in that year. The effect can be noted in chart 1.3. If one fits the 1870 exponential line for native born to age groups 20-24 and 45-69, he obtains rates almost as large as those in 1860. The war had a dramatic effect on the frequency pattern of foreign born. The modal class in 1870 effectively was be-tween 35 and 39 instead of 25 and 29 as in 1850 and 1860. The proportion of foreign-born adult males under 40 decreased from .65 and .66 in 1850 and 1860 to .56 in 1870. Only nonwhites in 1870 exhibited the apparent growth of the former years. This rate of $.048 - .017 = .031$ was similar to that of native-born free in 1850 and 1860.

No population analysis is offered at this point for areas of residence within the United States. I will consider the important comparisons among the Northeast, Northwest, and South in later chapters. It is useful, however, to examine the apparent growth rates as they have appeared (see table 1.2). The consistencies for native born are not found for foreign born. The latter values may differ from true long-run-trend figures by several points. The purpose in making the list is that findings in later chapters for wealth–age gradients seem to be roughly consistent with many of the figures in table 1.2. When wealth averages are plotted for various age groups in a given year, they show the old with more wealth than the young and apparent growth rates about 2 percent a year greater than for population growth. Various authorities, including Goldsmith and Kuznets,[5] have found long-run growth rates of wealth and income to be 1-2 percent a year. This suggests that actual per capita growth in wealth might be of this same general magnitude

Chart 1.3. Adult Males in Age Classes in the United States in 1870 by Nativity, Occupation, and Color

Number per year
of age (thousands)

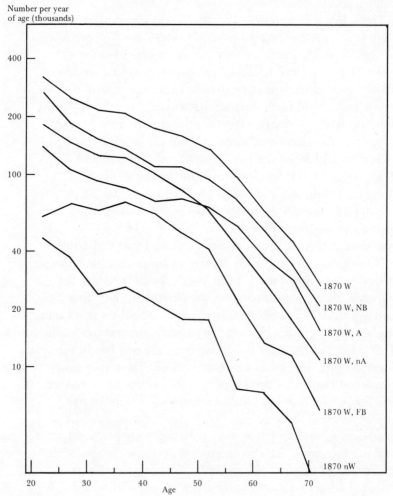

Source: See chart 1.1.

Table 1.2. Death-Inflated Rates of Apparent Population Growth for
Adult Males in 1850, 1860, and 1870

	1850 free[a]	*1860 free*	*1870 white*	*1870 all*
All	.030(.032)	.032(.035)	.025(.027)	.025(.027)
Farmers	.017	.022	.015(.019)	.018(.021)
Nonfarmers	.044	.044	.034(.035)	.034(.035)
Native born	.029	.029	.024(.028)	.026(.028)
Farmers	.018	.021	.017(.021)	.019(.023)
Nonfarmers	.043	.041	.034(.037)	.033(.035)
Foreign born	.038(.045)	.043(.053)	.027	.027
Farmers	.008(.018)	.030(.037)	.005	.005
Nonfarmers	.047(.054)	.050(.061)	.035	.035

Sources: Spin samples from schedules 1 of the 1850, 1860, and 1870
censuses of 10,393, 13,696, and 9,823.

Note: Each rate has been computed by fitting the semilogarithmic or
exponential equation to the death-inflated populations for ages 20–
69. Those in parentheses are for ages 25–69 in 1850 and 1860 and
20–24 and 45–69 in 1870.

[a]In 1850 farm laborers generally were not classified as farmers.

through *time* as manifested in our *age* data at specific points
in time.

Summary

We have found that the population of males 20 and older in
1850 and 1860 exhibited much greater proportions of young
in the United States than in other countries during that
period. The frequency distributions for ages of native-born
males in the two years were found to conform to the com-
pound-interest formula or exponential distribution with a
gradient of 4.5 percent per age year. Using chained annual
death rates, adjustment of this line for deaths yields a gradient of about 3 percent per year. This is probably about the
same as the long-run growth rate of native born after 1800
in this country. Thus, age in a given year does reflect time if
adjustment is made for deaths.

A similar analysis for occupations in 1850 and 1860 provides strong evidence that the number of adult male farmers and nonfarmers had been increasing at rates of about 2.2 and 4.4 percent a year in the nineteenth century. Furthermore, these rates were consistent with the rural–urban movement from 1860 to 1870 and, indeed, with current movement. The labor force did not suddenly become urban after the Civil War. The native-born difference in population–age gradients of $.045 - .016 = .029$, referred to above as the death effect, has significant theoretical importance in determining the per capita growth of wealth in the United States.

2. Who Held Property?

I limit myself in this chapter to a simple dichotomy of the
American population of the mid-nineteenth century: those
who held property and those who did not. Since property
was reported to the census taker in two forms—real and
personal—we examine here those who reported at least a
minimal holding in each of those categories in the censuses
of 1860 and 1870, in which both types were asked for.
The Census of 1850 unfortunately asked only for real
estate holdings, but in fact the distribution and conclusions
obtained by an analysis of the sample from that census
anticipate many of the main conclusions of the whole study.
Here, as later when we consider the distribution for size
classes of property holdings, it is possible to relate holders
of both classes of property to specific groups in the population by age, nativity, and occupation. We can examine personal property and total estate holders in the Censuses of
1860 and 1870 to show marginal modifications of the 1850
picture for the white population. Moreover, the methods of
analysis developed here carry over throughout our study.

I begin with simple summary results of the proportion of
men holding real and total estate in the study years. This
will be followed by an analysis of how these proportions
are related to the age, occupation, nativity, and residence
of individuals. Finally, I place my results for midcentury
within the broader perspective of general ownership participation rates since 1800. The 1850 and 1860 results provide
the link with the past; the 1870 information for free men
provides the link with the present.

Ownership Participation Rates

Propertyholder Proportion

Of the adult males 20 and over in 1850, slightly more than
40 percent (41.4%) held real property (PH = .414). From
the standpoint of owning a home or some land, the have-
nots substantially outnumbered the haves in the United
States. This fact should not be surprising, since the population of adult males consisted of disparate groups. Only half
were farmers even at this early date in development; the
remaining males could generally pursue their occupations
without owning land. It is true there were some farmers
and many urban dwellers who desired homes and other
property. But there were barriers to ownership such as inability to read and write English, general lack of knowledge
of the mechanism for obtaining land, absence of saving,
and lack of credit. One of every 10 adult males was
recorded as being unable to write in any language and
many more were only semiliterate.[1] Statistical data substantiate the obvious fact that illiterates were less likely
than literates to own land or homes.[2] There was an irreg-
ular stream of foreign born coming into the country, including many who desired to own farmland. One in every 5
men was foreign born in 1850; many of them had difficulty
in properly settling on land because of limited funds, un-
familiarity with American institutions and procedures for
acquiring land, and, in some cases, with the English language.[3]

One might present the thesis that the economy could
absorb only a certain proportion of nonpropertyholders at
a given time and that beyond this point danger signals would
arise that would stem the flow of immigrants. If this hypothesis were true, we would expect approximately the same
proportion of propertyholders in 1860 as in 1850, and in
1870 as in 1860. It is a remarkable fact that the property-

holder proportion for free men, PH, did *remain constant* for our three censuses, being .414 in 1850, .431 in 1860, and .433 for whites in 1870. These figures convey the impression that the economy was absorbing as many men as it could at any point in time for the economy to satisfy this theoretical minimum PH requirement of participation in capitalism. The only other specific PH the author knows of for any earlier year is that for Kentucky in 1800. The proportion of free males owning land, buildings, or lots was then .47, as opposed to .45 in 1850 and .46 in 1860.[4] Some international validation can be found in data for Ontario in 1871, which show PH of .47.[5] The average region in the United States had a PH of .45, but it is necessary to understand that there were differing PH values depending, often, on the relative importance of agriculture in each region. Perhaps a PH of about .45 was optimal in a typical region. If the proportion not participating (1 – PH) had risen substantially above .55, it would have constituted one of several signals that immigrants should go elsewhere and/or that individuals in the region should move farther west.

Total Estate Proportion

I turn next to sample results pertaining to holders of personal estate in the United States in 1860 and 1870. The proportion of adult men having personal estate of $100 or more was .576 in 1860 and .572 for whites in 1870.[6] It is reasonable to expect that these figures were larger than those for PH since movable goods, cash, stocks, and bonds encompass a wider choice of asset holdings than does the estate classification. However, it is the combination of real and personal property that is our most comprehensive measure of participation in wealthholding. Let us define the proportion of men with total estate of $100 or more as TEH. This proportion was .618 in 1860 and .616 for whites in 1870.

Evidence of stability in wealthholder participation in the United States is found in that 5 of each 8 adult males held $100 or more in 1860 and 1870. This finding is subject to several qualifications. The minimum dollar amount is arbitrarily imposed because smaller amounts were not recorded in 1870. The $100 might be considered to be the value either of 80 acres of land at the minimum price of $1.25 an acre or of one or two horses at prevailing prices. It was the equivalent of one-fifth of average annual income per worker in 1860. There were price increases from 1860 to 1870 that technically should be considered in connection with the $100 figure, but I will treat the amount as a minimum in each year. It also must be understood that inclusion of slaves or former slaves materially alters the figures. When nonwhites are included in the 1870 population, TEH is .57 instead of .62.[7]

Poor Men

The figures that have been cited are really quantifications of the poor rather than of the rich. I am not stating in this chapter merely how much wealth is owned by the have group; I am asserting only that the have-nots are very poor in terms of the assets they own. Roughly 3 in 8, or perhaps 1 in 3, had little more than clothing and possibly some petty cash. Undoubtedly some were younger men working on farms or in businesses belonging to their fathers but they can, at best, account for only 5-10 percent of the population.[8] It is probably not coincidence that various savings studies have shown that about one-third of individuals are unable to save during a year and that many have dissaving.[9] The majority of these persons come from low-income groups, which are dominated by individuals at the lower end of the scale of occupations. Those most subject to unemployment, particularly of a seasonal, as distinguished from a cyclical, nature, were common laborers. The number of farm laborers

Table 2.1. Number of Adult Males in the United States in 1860 with
Total Estate Less Than $100

	Age 20-29	*Age 30-99*
Native-born farmers	510,000	290,000
Foreign-born farmers	90,000	90,000
Native-born nonfarmers	580,000	420,000
Foreign-born nonfarmers	320,000	410,000
	1,500,000	1,210,000

Source: Spin sample of 13,696, drawn from the population of
7,100,000 free males aged 20 and older, of schedule 1 of the 1860
census.

and the number of day laborers represented about 20 percent of the population of all occupational groups in the
United States at this time and up to 40 percent of the stated
occupational populations of passengers arriving in the
United States.[10]

One would like to know how many of those with little or
no estate were young men, how many were in the rural sector of the economy, and how many were foreign born.
Table 2.1 gives us the necessary information for classifying
the 2.71 million poor men in the United States in 1860. It
is to be expected that over half the poor would be the
young from age 20 to 29 since more than one-third of all
adult males were in this age group and many of them would
not have had time to accumulate wealth. Nevertheless, it is
important to note that 40 percent of the young poor were
in the farm sector. This meant that these individuals had
yet to achieve ownership of land. There were almost equal
numbers of young native-born poor in rural and urban areas.

However, it is the propertyless aged 30 and over that
should be given the main attention. We see from table 2.1
that it was an urban and a foreign-born problem: two-
thirds of the poor lived in cities, three-sevenths of the poor
were foreign born, and half of the urban poor were foreign
born. Recent immigrants were known to possess little and

often had only small sums in cash, particularly after travel-
ing to their immediate destinations.[11] Social scientists observing the scene certainly knew of the foreign-born urban
problem but perhaps tended to minimize the problems of
the native born. Francis Bowen wrote in his *Principles of
Political Economy* in 1856 that "strictly speaking, we have
no poor except the vicious, and the recent immigrants."[12]
He felt that the United States was unique, even in contrast
to British America and Australia, in the ability of people
to save some money each year and start on the path to the
accumulation of wealth. "Neither theoretically nor prac-
tically, in this country, is there any obstacle to any individual's becoming rich, if he will, and almost to any
amount that he will;—no obstacle, I say, but what arises
from the dispensation of Providence, from the unequal
distribution of health, strength, and the faculties of mind."[13]

One wonders if Bowen would have retained this degree of
conviction in his beliefs if he actually had observed household conditions or even if he could have examined the
manuscript pages of the census of wealth in 1850 or 1860.
It is true that poor health was recognized and there must
have been some feeling for the probabilities of dying. Of
every 100 persons at age 20 in Massachusetts, there were
but 88 alive at age 30, and 69 who were still alive at age 50.[14]
But even the dying might inure one to the hardships of the
poor. If misfortune made the probability 1/3 that one would
not live 30 adult years, what was wrong with the misfortune
that made the probability 1/3 that one would have no
wealth? (Perhaps the death figures really are good proxies
for the deterioration in strength of the bodies of those living at the time.) Drunkenness was recognized as a problem,
as were insanity and infirmity.[15] But the infirm were but a
small percentage of the population as enumerated by the
census. Even today there are writers who feel that the poor
among native born essentially were not a problem of society
before the 1890s.[16] It is possible that a deprived group is

not readily recognized as such unless its language is distinct-
ly foreign or its color is not white.

The majority of writers felt that initiative and self-help
were really the important ingredients of society and that
only the small proportion of paupers should be helped.
Depressions, the crushing impact of seasonal unemployment, and general poor health apparently were not recognized as problems of society before the 1870s, 1880s, or
1890s. My findings for 1850, 1860, and 1870, as illustrated
in part by table 2.1, are that there were poor before the
Civil War and that they were not all immigrants. Indeed,
there were more native born than foreign born who were
poor.

Age

The strength of America's system, as seen by nineteenth-
century writers, was that an individual had the opportunity
to improve his position over time. This opportunity meant
that he was not placed in a fixed position in society. He
might have had to work hard, but he could expect betterment in his wealth status. We can capture this phenomenon
by studying the participation rate of peoples of different
ages in a given year. Surely this rate, as measured by PH or
TEH, must be higher for the old than for the young. A person might always remain a nonfarmer, he necessarily must
remain foreign born, he might always in adult life have the
same religion, ethnicity, and educational level, but at least
his age will change with time.

Obviously, age has great bearing on the probability of
owning property. If the majority of individuals in an economy are to experience betterment in economic position
during their lifetimes, more and more should rise above the
level of being poor, above some minimum wealth amount.
My statistics allow us to measure change with age in the
participation of people in accumulation.

Property Ownership in 1850

The proportion holding property, PH, would be very small at age 20 or 21 and would be expected to increase with age in some methodical fashion. This PH pattern for 1850 plotted in chart 2.1 shows a very rapid rise in the probability of ownership in the first 10 years of adulthood with a tapering effect appearing thereafter. The increase for all the years after age 40 is essentially no more than that occurring in the first 10-year period.

The shape is undoubtedly influenced in part by an income or saving distribution, and there *is* a semblance of a "more than" cumulative frequency curve in chart 2.1. The interpretation might be that only the upper-income group would have saving sufficient to obtain property at a young age; middle-income groups could save sufficient sums after a series of years that might roughly reach the median-income group among those who were 40 years of age. It would be difficult for the bottom third—with less than modal incomes—to save. I am describing only a general tendency since it is obvious that at a specific age there are some with low income who are property owners and some with high income who do not have property.

One can present an argument that there is a consistency between the PH levels at various ages if one uses the probability figures in the accompanying table.

Age	Actual PH	Theoretical calculation approximating PH using .207
20-29	.207	$1 - (.793) = .207$
30-39	.453	$1 - (.793)^2 = .371$
40-49	.571	$1 - (.793)^3 = .501$
50-59	.604	$1 - (.793)^4 = .605$
60-69	.660	$1 - (.793)^5 = .686$

The PH of .207 may be interpreted as the probability of obtaining property from age 20 to 29; its complement of $1 - .207$, or .793, may be considered the probability of not

Chart 2.1. Proportion of Adult Free Males Having Real Estate (PH) and Total Estate (TEH)

PH or TEH

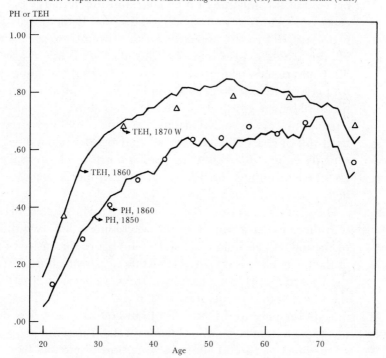

Sources: Spin samples of 1850, 1860, and 1870. The lines are 5-year moving averages.

obtaining property. The theoretical series would be generated if this latter probability persisted in later age periods.

The .793 is a quantification of the importance of all those
characteristics inhibiting ownership, such as lack of knowledge of available land or credit, inability to speak or write
English or possibly to read any other language, unwilling-
ness to accept the obligations of ownership, inability to save
because of low income or high consumption, lethargy because of sickness or poor health, and so on. If the quantification of .793 were to operate for the group from age 30 to
39, one would expect that .793 of the propertyless at age
30 would remain propertyless. Thus, $1 - (.793)^2$ would own
property in the 30-39 group. Application of the same princi-
ple to older age groups leads to the series above. It generates
a parabolic curve somewhat similar to the actual PH curve
for 1850 of chart 2.1. This means that the entire curve is
roughly consistent with its beginning portion. The causal
factors determining inability to acquire property seem to
be consistent through a fairly large range.[17]

The process operates, at best, to age 70. The highest PH
is in the age class from 65 to 69, where more than two-thirds
of the individuals held real estate. The figure for native born
in the latter class was .700, consisting of persons born in
the United States from 1780 to 1789 who became 20 after
the year 1800. It seems strange that 3 of every 10 whites
born in the period of the birth of our country were destined
not to own homes, land, or business establishments.

One must be careful about making time inferences from
age when he has data for only one year. The figures may
very well not represent adequately the experience of a given
individual or group of individuals during their *lifetimes*. If
PH is a function of time as well as of age at one point in
time, it is difficult to isolate the two effects. Consider our
PH proportion curve for 1850 in chart 2.1. The line for
1820 could have been above it at all ages or below it at all
ages. It could have been above if the economy were more

predominantly rural or native born or below if frontier land
were relatively inaccessible because of lack of transportation,
communication, or credit facilities or because of the threat
of Indians. If the curve for 1820 lay below that for 1850,
the age cohort, which was 30-34 in 1820 and 60-64 in 1850,
would have had a PH proportion curve rising less rapidly in
early age and more rapidly in later age years than does the
1850 curve.

There seems, however, to be a certain consistency in the
PH proportion curve and population growth at the time,
which implies a fixed PH curve over time. A second-degree
equation fitted to the points[18] has the form PH = $-.633 +$
$.044$ age $- .00037$(age)^2. We can calculate the increase in PH
from the average age of 37 in 1850 to that a year later at
38. This raises PH by 3.2 percent, which almost matches
the annual increase in population in the United States at
the time. There is some implication that the curve would
have risen over time if the increase had been much greater
than 3.2 percent.

Property Ownership in 1860 and 1870

Fortunately we can check the stability in the participation index by calculating PH in 1860 and 1870. Chart 2.1
shows that the parabolic pattern for PH in 1860 is almost
identical to that in 1850. Table 2.2 will show that the pattern is faithfully reproduced again for whites in 1870. The
annual change in PH may be estimated by applying the
average age and 1 plus the average age to a fitted parabola.[19]
This calculation indicates an increase in PH of slightly more
than 3 percent a year in 1850, 1860, and 1870. If population increased about 3 percent a year, we would expect the
lines to remain in the same position, other things being the
same. Given my parabolas, suppose a population were growing by only 2 percent. One could then expect a shift upward in the curve in the decade since the number already

in the labor force obtaining property in the year would be
larger than the number of new entrants. I will discuss possible effects counteracting that of age in the sections on
occupation and nativity.

Wealthholder Proportions

Two features of the proportion of men holding total
estate of $100 or more (TEH), as depicted in chart 2.1, are
of interest. Note that there is stability in the pattern for
the decade of study since the TEH configuration for 1860
is very similar to that for whites in 1870. The TEH curve
lies substantially above that for propertyholders (PH) because it includes individuals with personal estate who were
not real propertyholders, a group constituting 20 percent
of the population. The total estate proportion rises from
.40 for those in their twenties to .68 for those in their
thirties to .78 for those 40 or older. The curve rises above
.80 in some ranges so that we can say something about
what an average American could anticipate. The probability
would be 80 percent that at some time in his life he would
rise above our arbitrary level of poverty assets. Conversely,
the curve for poverty (1 – TEH) starts very high among the
young and decreases at a decreasing absolute rate to about
20 percent.

I will explore implications of economic growth in the
1860 curve. Perhaps over the long run one would find that
greater and greater proportions of people at a given age
would have estates of more than $100 in real terms. It
might be expected that the TEH curve would shift upward
in succeeding decades and that the curve a century later
would show a fairly small percentage who are poor. The
fact that the 1870 curve definitely did not lie above and
probably lay below the 1860 curve would have to be attributed to the war, cyclical conditions, and underevalua-
tion.[20]

Table 2.2. Male Holders of Real Estate Aged 20 and Older (PH) in
the United States in 1850, 1860, and 1870, by Age,
Nativity, and Occupation, as a Proportion of the Male
Population in Each Class

	Age			
	20 and up	*20-29*	*30-39*	*40-99*
1850 free				
All persons	.414	.21	.45	.60
Native born	.450	.23	.50	.64
Foreign born	.245	.08	.26	.40
Farmers[a]	.607	.34	.66	.77
Native born	.603	.35	.65	.77
Foreign born	.664	.32	.76	.77
Nonfarmers[a]	.259	.12	.32	.39
Native born	.298	.15	.38	.44
Foreign born	.146	.05	.18	.24
1860 free				
All persons	.431	.21	.45	.63
Native born	.469	.22	.50	.68
Foreign born	.324	.16	.35	.46
Farmers	.569	.28	.60	.77
Native born	.572	.28	.60	.78
Foreign born	.550	.28	.60	.70
Nonfarmers	.297	.14	.33	.45
Native born	.339	.16	.39	.51
Foreign born	.218	.11	.24	.31
1870 whites only				
All persons	.433	.18	.45	.62
Native born	.465	.20	.49	.68
Foreign born	.351	.13	.36	.48
Farmers	.582	.27	.63	.77
Native born	.574	.27	.61	.78
Foreign born	.631	.29	.71	.73
Nonfarmers	.307	.12	.33	.46
Native born	.338	.13	.37	.53
Foreign born	.258	.09	.27	.37

Sources: Spin samples from schedules 1 of the 1850, 1860, and
1870 censuses of 10,393, 13,696, and 9,823, respectively.

[a]In 1850 farm laborers generally were not classified as farmers.

The 1860 configuration may be characterized almost exactly by use of the least-squares equation TEH = $-.714 +$ .048 age $-$ .00041(age)^2. If we compute the annual change in TEH by applying the population at each age to the TEH one year later, we find the rather surprising result that TEH increases less than 3 percent. This would mean that TEH would remain relatively stable in the face of population increases of about 2-3 percent. The idea that the proportion who were poor, 1 – TEH, would remain constant in the decades following 1860 is somewhat shocking. The implication at this point is based solely on the TEH–age parabolas for 1860 and 1870. It is possible that the rural–urban movement could act as a deterrent to an upward shift, and we turn next to an examination of this variable.

Occupation

It is to be expected that there was greater wealth participation among farm groups than among urban groups. This is particularly true for the real property category since farmers and farm laborers generally aspire to own their farms. Most city workers may aspire, at best, to own homes. The magnitude of the difference between the PH and TEH ratios for farmers and nonfarmers is strategic in estimating the impact of the rural–urban movement, particularly in the nineteenth century. One might expect urbanization to produce enlargement of the poverty class and alienation of larger portions of society if differences in these variables for occupational categories are large.

Figures for real estate participation are given in table 2.2 for the three census years of the study. The focus is the categories for farmers and nonfarmers, where values were about twice as high for the one group as the other, as the following table shows. The 1860 and 1870 figures are very similar and might, for practical purposes, be considered to be the same. The 1850 proportions probably would be

	1850	1860	1870 whites
PH, farmers	.61	.57	.58
PH, nonfarmers	.26	.30	.31

nearly the equivalent of those in 1860 if we could properly
adjust them to the 1860 definition of *farmer*. There is a
statistical problem with the 1850 figures because farm
laborers were classified only as laborers and so were necessarily included in the nonfarm category for that year. One
way to make 1850-1860 comparisons is to deal only with
propertyholders; by this means, all farm *laborers* are eliminated from consideration. I then found that the proportion
of all propertyholders who were farmers was exactly the
same in the two years (.652). Thus, I feel that PH for farm
and nonfarm groups remained quite stable for the three
census years.[21]

The classifications for total estate place urban groups in
a much better light since sizable numbers of urban dwellers
who held no real estate nevertheless had personal estate of
more than $100. Findings are given in the accompanying
table.

	1860	1870 whites
TEH, farmers	.72	.74
TEH, nonfarmers	.52	.51

We see that half of adult men in cities are deemed poor
whereas only one-quarter of adult men in rural areas fall in
this category. The situation is much more poignant in cities,
where the have-nots are as numerous as the haves. It could
be maintained that the have-nots were able to function
because the haves provided the necessary employment
opportunities by investing their wealth in productive trade
and manufacturing. On the other hand it could be argued
that the haves were able to obtain their wealth because the
have-nots supplied the necessary labor.

Most major urban areas of the United States had poor in
greater numbers than did the country as a whole. For

example, instead of half of adult males having wealth less
than $100 in 1860, New York City had 1 – TEH of .63,
while the proportions were .62 for Boston and .59 for Philadelphia. Cities farther west apparently were better off since
1 – TEH values were .51 in Chicago and .43 in Milwaukee
for the same year.[22] These data provide evidence that there
was not immediate movement of peoples at the lowest end
of the income spectrum to those areas allowing accumulation of assets. The census figures do confirm the general
impressions of social historians that there were masses of
adult males in America's largest cities who were poor.
Such historians may not have emphasized that this condition existed prior to, as well as after, the Civil War. I estimate that 15 percent of America's poor of 1860 (see table
2.1) were located in the 10 largest northern cities. It is not
surprising that 5 percent of America's poor were in New
York City, since it comprised 3 percent of the adult male
population. The finding that half of the urban born owned
no wealth was also obtained in Yankee City in the early
1930s. W. Lloyd Warner's lower class encompassed a lower-
lower and upper–lower group, each of which had essentially
no wealth. This could be true because his study was made
during the Great Depression and because a rigid minimum
wealth figure was not stipulated.[23] Our poor now take on
more meaning in terms of social classes found by researchers
in urban areas of the United States in the twentieth century.

Nativity

The census chronicles a strong and pervasive difference in
the minimum asset holdings of nativity groups. It is clear
that there were relatively more poor among foreign born
than among native born, and we may speak of a foreign-
born handicap or gap. The proportion holding property in
1850 was .45 among native born and .25 among foreign
born. It is true that this gap was narrowed to .47 – .32 in

1860 and to .47 - .35 for whites in 1870. The handicap is
based on the fact that foreign born were less able to cope
with factors and institutions in the United States relating to
saving, inheritance, and wealth accumulation.

There were definite language barriers that were particularly
crucial for those not knowing English. A factor of consequence was inability to read and write in any language, a
handicap especially important in understanding the plight
of the poor. The proportion of adult men and women in
1860 who were unable to read and write was twice as high
in one group as in the other, being 14.6 percent for foreign-
born and 7.6 percent for native-born whites. There were
1.28 million free adult persons in the United States in 1860
recorded as being unable to write.[24] There must have been
many more whose writing abilities were very faulty. How
could these individuals be adept in the use of financial and
legal documents and notices pertaining to the purchase of
farms or homes?

A second major handicap was the previous background
of the foreign born, and, more particularly, those within
the group who were poor. They may have been in the
United States only a few years;[25] several or many of their
adult years may have been spent in areas of a foreign
country where the probability of acquiring any assets was
extremely small.

A third factor was inheritance since we know that the
chances of receiving property from abroad were very small.
Effectively, all foreign born had parents who were foreign
born and, conversely, the vast majority (over 80 percent)
of the native born had native-born parents.[26] One may
apply death rate estimates for 1860 to our PH parabolas of
1850 and 1860 to determine that more than half the deceased males in the United States died with property and
three-fourths had estates of at least $100. This would
provide some flow of wealth to children.

The data of table 2.3 allow us to examine in detail the

Table 2.3. Male Holders of Total Estate (TEH) in the United States
           in 1860 and 1870, by Age, Nativity, and Occupation, as
           a Proportion of the Male Population in Each Class

		Age		
	20 and up	*20-29*	*30-39*	*40-99*
		1860 free		
All persons	.618	.40	.68	.78
Native born	.658	.43	.73	.82
Foreign born	.505	.32	.57	.62
Farmers	.720	.48	.78	.87
Native born	.726	.48	.79	.88
Foreign born	.687	.46	.74	.80
Nonfarmers	.519	.34	.59	.66
Native born	.572	.37	.66	.73
Foreign born	.420	.27	.49	.51
		1870 whites		
All persons	.616	.38	.69	.76
Native born	.655	.41	.75	.82
Foreign born	.516	.27	.59	.62
Farmers	.742	.46	.82	.87
Native born	.744	.50	.82	.89
Foreign born	.731	.42	.83	.80
Nonfarmers	.510	.29	.60	.65
Native born	.550	.31	.67	.71
Foreign born	.445	.24	.52	.54
		1870 all		
All persons	.569	.34	.65	.71
Native born	.586	.36	.67	.77
Foreign born	.515	.27	.58	.62
Farmers	.659	.42	.73	.79
Native born	.649	.42	.71	.79
Foreign born	.727	.42	.82	.80
Nonfarmers	.484	.27	.58	.61
Native born	.507	.29	.63	.66
Foreign born	.444	.23	.51	.55

Sources: Spin samples of 13,696 and 9,823 from schedules 1 of the
1860 and 1870 censuses, respectively.

foreign-born handicap for total wealth. The TEH gap of
.658-.505 indicates that two-thirds of native born, contrasted to one-half of foreign born, were above the wealth
level of $100. Nevertheless, the figures indicate that there
was essentially no gap in rural areas between the two nativity
groups. It was centered in the *urban* areas, where the probability of ownership was 10 to 15 percent higher for native
born than for foreign born (.57-.42).

Examination of the TEH values for different age groups
shows that parabolic shapes were maintained for specific
nativity and occupation groups. In other words the age pattern pervaded all other classifications of the data, although
absolute differences in age parabolas did increase a little
with age: the foreign-born gap among nonfarmers was
.37-.27 for those 20-29 and .73-.51 for those over 40. The
data of table 2.3 may be generalized by fitting a multiple
regression line to the data for all the men in the sample;
the data may be formulated: TEH = $-.490 + .054$ age $-$
$.0005$ age^2 $- .154$ nA $- .120$ FB. Here nA is given the value
of 1 for nonfarmers and 0 for farmers; likewise, the category FB is 1 for foreign born and 0 for native born.[27] This
additive model may be interpreted to mean that, given a
certain age and nativity, the probability is 15.4 percent less
that an individual would have wealth of $100 or more if he
is a nonfarmer rather than a farmer. The probability is 12.0
percent less that he will hold minimum wealth if he is foreign
born instead of native born. The unfortunate individual who
is both foreign born and urban has his probability of wealthholding cut by 27 percent. But both these factors do not
have the impact of the pervasive age variable.

Table 2.3 also reveals that the configurations for the
variables occupation, nativity, and age are very similar for
1860 and for whites in 1870. A glance at the column for
those 40-99 shows that ratios for nine comparable categories in the two years do not differ by more than 1-3 points
and are identical for four of the comparisons. I offer the

TEH values for *all* persons, both white and nonwhite in
1870, in table 2.3 because such values would be the ones
most directly comparable with twentieth-century data. The
foreign-born gap and the urban gap are not so readily apparent for all in 1870. The explanation is that former slaves
were native born and most often located in the farm sector.
There is 1870 evidence for the *farm* sector that foreign
born in the United States were more likely than native born
to be holders of capital! Later I will make a comparison
between the proportion of people with wealth in 1870 and
its counterpart in 1962-63. Since it will be an economy
dominated almost entirely by native-born nonfarmers who
are substantially older, we will be focusing on the table 2.3
values of those 30-39 and 40-99 in these categories, namely,
the TEH entries of .63-.66. One wonders if one-third of the
people in this country are poor even now.

Residence and Birth Regions

The three main variables of this study are age, nativity, and
occupation. A fourth significant variable is the state or
region of the country in which the individual lived. Combina-
tions of the first three variables inevitably result in regional
differences in PH and TEH. Regions with relatively older
men, relatively more farmers, and relatively more native
born should be those with higher rates of propertyholding
and wealthholding. These results are borne out by the figures in table 2.4.

Characteristics in 1850

To make regional comparisons of wealth distribution,
the states and territories were divided into nine regions with
the slaveholding South constituting one of the nine. Table
2.4 shows values for freemen only of several of our study
variables for these regions. Note that the average age of adult

Table 2.4. Characteristics of Free Adult Males in the Various Regions of Residence in the United States in 1850, including Population Size, Age, Nativity, Occupation, and the Proportion Holding Real Estate (PH)

	Share of total population in the U.S. (1)	Average age (2)	Proportion foreign born (3)	Proportion farmer (4)	Proportion holding property (PH)		
					All (5)	farmers (6)	Non-farmers (7)
1. Me., N.H., Vt.	.06	39	.09	.53	.53	.71	.33
2. Conn., Mass., R.I.	.08	39	.18	.21	.32	.63	.24
3. N.Y., N.J.	.19	37	.30	.32	.31	.59	.18
4. Pa.	.11	37	.20	.32	.39	.61	.28
5. Ohio	.09	37	.17	.51	.47	.58	.36
6. Ind., Ill., Mich.	.10	36	.18	.63	.54	.65	.35
7. Wis., Ia., Dak.	.03	36	.38	.60	.52	.69	.25
8. West[a]	.02	30	.17	.11	.18	.48	.14
9. South[b]	.30	36	.10	.54	.43	.57	.27
All	1.00	37	.18	.44	.41	.61	.26
North (1-8)	.70	37	.22	.40	.41	.63	.26
Northeast (1-4)	.46	37	.22	.33	.36	.63	.24
Northwest (5-8)	.24	33	.20	.54	.48	.63	.32

Source: Spin samples of 10,393 from schedule 1 of the 1850 census.

[a]West, nonslave states: Cal., Kan., Ore., Col., Neb., Nev., N.M., Utah, and Wash.
[b]South, slave states: Del., Md., Va., W.Va., Ky., Mo., Ark., Tex., and Southeast.

males decreases as one moves west from regions 1 and 2 in New England, through region 3 of New York–New Jersey, to 4 of Pennsylvania and 5 of Ohio, to 6 in Indiana–Illinois–

Michigan, 7 in Wisconsin–Iowa–Dakota, and 8 in nonslave areas farther west. Because these last two regions have small populations and sample sizes, they might have been combined for this study except for the fact that their characteristics show sharp enough differences, which come through in the statistics, to warrant their being separate.

I consider first the proportion of propertyholders (PH) in each region by observing how much it differs from the average (.41) for the country as a whole. Excluding northern New England with its widespread land ownership and the Far West with very little (PH = .18), one finds a clear gradient in moving west from region 2 to region 7. The probability of ownership is two-thirds again as large in the agricultural Middle West as it is in the East. A large part of this situation is due to the greater proportion of farmers in the regional populations as one moves west. The PH values for farmers (col. 6) in regions 2–7 vary only between .58 and .69, and there is a rough correspondence between the PH measure (col. 5) and the proportion of farmers in the population (col. 4).

Regional differences are most influenced by the occupation dichotomy but the differences in nativity and average age also have an effect on the differences. The relationship between nativity and longitude is less clear than that between age and longitude. Regions 3 (N.Y., N.J.) and 7 (Wis., Ia., Dak.) have substantially higher proportions of foreign born than the others (col. 3); this 1850 pattern is found to continue in 1860 and 1870. The midcentury frontier, then, has a population both relatively young and with a higher proportion of recent immigrants, which help explain its relatively low proportion of propertyholders. Even so, a young man's probability of being a propertyholder might be greater there than in the East. We would need to know how a given individual would perform in both regions or to compare how individuals graded by ability were able to perform in either the old or the new

regions. But no reliable evidence is available to answer the
question: Was it the weak or the strong who moved west?
A certain degree of data control is possible for the available
information on some characteristics of men in both regions,
such as age, nativity, and occupation. Adjustments for these
factors can be made using procedures of standardization or
multiple regression.[28] Results indicate clearly the positive
relationship between ownership probability and western
settlement.

Characteristics in 1860 and 1870

Regional differences in holder proportions in 1860 and
1870 were generally the same as those in 1850. However,
there is some evidence that a region's participation in ownership proceeded in a curvilinear fashion through three stages.
The levels of PH and TEH might have been fairly low in the
initial decades of settlement; then they may have increased
to a level above that in settled states as land purchases were
made in an efficient manner in the midst of settlement.
Finally, the level would drop as acreage of unsettled and unimproved land became rather limited in the state or region.
I found that region 6 (Ind., Ill., Mich.) had a drop in PH
from 1850 to 1860, reverting to a level like that of Ohio.
The increase for region 7 (Wis., Ia., Dak.) in this period
was substantial, with the level rising beyond that of region
6 in 1850. This curvilinear pattern was found in a county
analysis for Wisconsin at midcentury.[29]

The Northwest states (Ohio and west) continue to show
a better overall record than the South or Northeast in the
proportion of men who held real property and wealth. This
was particularly true in urban areas, as shown by the nonfarm group in the accompanying table. However, the urban
movement from 1860 to 1870 did *not* essentially alter any
of the regional values in PH and TEH.

| | PH, 1860 | | | TEH, 1860 | | |
	All	*Farmer*	*Non-farmer*	*All*	*Farmer*	*Non-farmer*
Northeast	.38	.56	.28	.57	.66	.51
Northwest	.48	.59	.35	.64	.73	.53
South	.43	.56	.27	.66	.76	.52

Countries of Birth

The few texts on economics written during our study period stressed the numbers of foreign labor performing menial jobs. One would expect the Irish, who formed the supply for common labor, to have low PH and TEH. Irish labor apparently was cheapest and "the first thrown out in a reduction."[30] There were 730,000 foreign-born men in urban areas in the United States in 1860 who had less than $100 in wealth (see table 2.1). Of these poor, the 54 percent of Irish birth constituted more than half the foreign-born poor and one-fifth of all poor in America's urban areas. For the country as a whole they represented 1 of every 10 among the population of men, but half again as many among its poor men.

It is not surprising that Irish immigrants are at the bottom of the list of birth groups in terms of owning property. The PH values by country of birth for 1860 were .24 for Ireland, .37 for Germany, .41 for England, Scotland, and Wales, and .47 for the United States. These figures indicate that the probability of an Irishman's owning a farm or home was but half as large as that of a native-born individual. In the case of total estate the TEH values in 1860 by country of birth were .42 for Ireland, .57 for Germany, .59 for England, Scotland, and Wales, and .66 for the United States. It is true that the Irish handicap is less apparent in the urban sector, where the TEH is .36 for the Irish and .57 for the native born.

Residence Related to Birth

The census manuscripts include the state or territory of birth of each native-born resident. These data give important clues about the westward movement for any residence region such as Ohio, Illinois, or Iowa. One wonders if those born in New York and living in Illinois might have done better if they had remained in New York or whether they might have done better yet by moving to Iowa. Would those born in Ohio have prospered more by moving to Illinois or by remaining in Ohio? In this chapter betterment is treated from the standpoint of whether someone meets a minimum standard of owning property or wealth. It would surely seem that those born in the Northeast would be more likely to escape being poor by migrating to the Northwest with its relatively abundant land and employment opportunities.

My hypothesis of fewer poor in the Northwest (Ohio and west) is clearly established from the statistics in the accompanying table.[31]

	Northeast birth	
	PH	*TEH*
Northeast residence	.44	.62
Northwest residence	.57	.73

It may be argued that the difference reflects only that those who desired to move were farmers rather than urban workers. The 11-point regional difference in poor for TEH becomes a still substantial 7-point difference if we adjust the data for differences in occupation and age (Appendix tables A1 and A2). This may have been the only real regional premium necessary to get the poor people to move from the eastern part of the country. It is seen in table A2 that the same regional premium existed among foreign born. At least one economist at the time bemoaned the fact that people deserted the urban East with its productive urban

activities. He argued that the country needed some proper
proportion of rural and urban life if it were to expand most
advantageously and that free land would tend to distort
this theoretical ratio.[32] The PH differentials presumably
would have been substantially higher than they were.

Deprived Groups since 1800

Literature abounds with the idea that the rich got richer in
the last half of the nineteenth century, but there is some
question about the status of the poor. G. P. Watkins reported at length on the "growth of large fortunes" in the
publications of the American Economic Association in
1907. He quoted with approval a statement of James Bryce:
"Sixty years ago there were no great fortunes in America,
few large fortunes, and no poverty. Now there is some
poverty, many large fortunes, and a greater number of
gigantic fortunes than in any other country of the world."[33]
Carroll D. Wright, commissioner of labor and one time chief
of the census, wrote in 1897 that the rich were getting richer
but that the poor were becoming better off.[34] There was
uncertainty about what was happening to deprived groups.

   We need some fundamental knowledge about the number
of those without property and wealth and how it has
changed in the last century if we are to understand the extent of participatory democracy. The remaining sections of
this chapter are largely devoted to this subject. So far I have
described conditions of minimum ownership among the
poor in 1850-70. A projection of poor from 1870 to 1960
will be made on the basis of demographic data for our three
important independent variables. I will compare the results
with home ownership figures and the Federal Reserve study
in 1962, which gives data on the proportion of families with
little or no wealth. This will be followed by a discussion of
Negroes before and after the Civil War and of poor whites
from 1800 to the Civil War.

Projections of Participation Rates

Many people have the impression that the relative number of poor increased after the Civil War because of urbanization and possibly also because of immigration. Table 2.3 shows that the proportion holding total estate of .57 for all adult males in 1870 was composed of figures of .66 for farmers and .48 for nonfarmers. It must seem readily apparent that the relative movement of men to cities would increase the number of poor to about half the population. More specifically, farmers dropped from half the population in 1870 to 8 percent of it in 1960. The TEH for 1960, estimated on the basis of 1960 occupation and 1870 TEH for all men, would then be .08(.66) + .92(.48), or .50. The number of men with wealth would drop from 57 to 50 per 100 because of the urban movement.[35] This is not so substantial as one would expect for several reasons. First, the fact that there were many poor farmers, including those who formerly had been slaves, made our occupational differential only 18 percentage points. Second, there were so many without wealth a century ago. This is a reiteration of the central finding that there were so many poor, even in farm areas. It was not true that every farmer had wealth and that every nonfarmer did not.

Some would assert that the significant immigration before 1920 would account for increasing numbers of poor. The TEH for all men in 1870 showed a nativity differential of .59 - .52. The percentage of adult men who were foreign born was 25 in 1870, remained 24 to 25 in each census year from 1880 to 1910, and then dropped to 8 in 1960. The main point is that the trend in the foreign-born proportion gives us no basis for saying that the relative number of poor would increase from the Civil War to World War I. The drop in foreign born by 1960 would lead to a slightly higher projected TEH value in 1960 of .58.

Our next consideration is the important variable, age.

The average age of adult men rose in development of this country from 37 in 1850 to 45 in 1960. This has a great influence in lowering the proportion of poor since the probability of accumulating minimum wealth increases with age. One may calculate a projected TEH for 1960 on the basis of age by applying the populations of the age groups 20-29, 30-39, and 40-99 in 1960 to the TEH values for these three groups given in table 2.3. When this is done, one obtains a projected TEH of .62, a figure 5 percent larger than the value in 1870! It is quite possible that the aging of the population would be a positive factor in lessening the number of poor to a degree that would counteract the negative force generated by the urban movement.

The magnitude of the 1960 TEH projection, based on TEH values for all men in 1870 and on 1960 population weights, is .50 for occupation, .58 for nativity, .62 for age, and .58 for all three variables.[36] The projected 1960 value of .58 is about the same as the actual 1870 PH of .57. The aging of the population and, to a much smaller extent, the decrease in immigration counteracted the increase in urbanization. I will give evidence shortly that actual TEH in 1960 may have been 10 percent *larger* than the projected value. There is some evidence that urban groups particularly have had increased probabilities of ownership beyond those projected.

Let us try one more projection in order to gain some insight into what might have occurred to the number of adult males with homes in the period from 1850 to 1980. The constancy in the PH–age parabolas in 1850-1870 tempts us to apply age-specific population weights from each census to the PH of various age groups in 1870 shown in the accompanying table.

PH

1850	.370	1880	.388	1910	.400	1940	.429	1970	.438
1860	.376	1890	.393	1920	.414	1950	.439	1980	.423
1870	.391	1900	.397	1930	.422	1960	.455		

This series varies only because of changes in age composition from one decade to another. It is interesting that there
is little change from 1870 to after 1910. The period from
1920 to 1960 would be one of increased ownership; there
would then be a rapid reversion back to the level of the
earlier period because of large increases in the number of
youths. I give some verification of the projections in the
next section.

Home Ownership from 1890 to 1960

There are statistics on homeownership, beginning with
the Census of 1890, that come close to embodying our
concept of the propertyholder and, therefore, give us a
perspective on a century of ownership participation. If we
divide the number of adult males holding property by the
number of families rather than by the number of adult
males, we can approximate the homeownership proportion
of later years. The number of families reported in 1870 was
77 percent of the number of adult males. If the PH values
for all males, farmers, and nonfarmers are each divided by
.77, family-adjusted PHs of .51, .65, and .38, respectively,
are obtained. These estimates of homeownership are remarkably similar to their counterpart homeowner proportions in
1890 of .48, .66, and .37. Any differences could be attributed, in the main, to owners not occupying their homes.
The similarities for the two years are taken as substantial
evidence that the proportion of poor in the country remained essentially constant in the 20 years after 1870 and
that the projections made previously are verified. Recall
that the PH parabola arising from the study of age in 1850
and 1860 indicates that the number of men obtaining
property in a year matched the increase in population in
that year.

Homeowner data for succeeding decades have now added
meaning, and one can examine with interest the movements

Table 2.5. Owner-Occupied Dwelling Units as a Proportion of All
Occupied Dwelling Units, as Reported for 1890-1960 and
Estimated for 1850-70

	All	Farm	Nonfarm
Estimated			
1850[a]	.50	–	–
1860[a]	.52	–	–
1870	.51	.65	.38
Census data			
1890	.48	.66	.37
1900	.47	.64	.37
1910	.46	.63	.38
1920	.46	.58	.41
1930	.48	.54	.46
1940	.44	.53	.41
1950	.55	.66	.53
1960	.62	.74[b]	.61[b]
1970	.63	–	–

Source: U.S. Bureau of the Census, *Historical Statistics of the United
States, Colonial Times to 1957* (Washington, D.C.: GPO, 1960),
series A 255, N 139-146, K 8-52. The estimating procedure for 1850-
70, using spin-sample data, is described in the text.

Note: Dash indicates data not available.

[a] Using adult male populations adjusted to include slaves with no
ownership.
[b] Not comparable with earlier data.

shown in table 2.5. It is seen that the ownership proportion
remained basically constant from 1890 to 1940 and that it
probably was constant for at least a century prior to World
War II. There is evidence after 1900 that the constancy was
a composite of ownership improvement in the urban sector
and decline in the farm sector. This demonstrates that urban
income was improving for middle groups. The rapid increase
after World War II is more dramatic evidence that income
was rising for the whole middle third of income recipients.
The overall ownership trend is not dissimilar to that of the
PH projection given in the previous section for 1890-1960.

Table 2.6. Proportion of Adult Males with Property (PH) in 1860
and 1870 and the Proportion of Families Owning Homes
in 1962-63 Classified by Age

Age	PH in 1860, nonslaves	PH in 1870, all	Homeowner proportion 1962-63
Under 35	.27	.22	.34
35-44	.53	.47	.57
45-54	.64	.56	.69
55-64	.68	.62	.67
65 and up	.61	.60	.61
All	.43	.39	.57

Sources: Spin samples of 13,696 and 9,823 from 1860 and 1870;
Dorothy S. Projector and Gertrude S. Weiss, *Survey of Financial
Characteristics of Consumers,* Federal Reserve Technical Papers
(Washington, D.C.: Federal Reserve Board, 1966), pp. 110, 171.

That projection was based on change in age composition
of the population and there is no doubt that it is a major
factor.[37]

   The homeowner figures given in table 2.6 for 1962-63,
based on a study by the Federal Reserve Board, indicate
that the age gradient is generally present today as it was in
1870. The difference in the proportions for the two years
is roughly 10 percent for specific age groups even though
the difference for all groups is substantially larger. This is
true because the population was substantially older in
1962-63. The table indicates that age-specific ownership
today is not much more than it was for whites in 1860.
This is one way of measuring the extent of improvement
in propertyholding in the United States during the century.
One should not emphasize the findings from statistics on
homeownership unduly, since purchases today are a function of many institutional factors not immediately determined by economic conditions.

The Poor Today and a Century Ago

Table 2.1 gives figures for the number of poor among the free population of the United States in 1860. It is of historical interest to compare the frequency of their numbers for that year with that reported in the Federal Reserve Study for 1962-63. Such a comparison will allow us some perspective on the magnitude of change in poverty during the century. The evidence presented in the previous section pertained only to the failure of individuals to obtain real estate, not total estate. A measure of total estate or wealth is needed since individuals today can hold minimum assets in a variety of forms. We hope, at best, to have a time index for failure of men to participate in accumulation under capitalism; it is admitted that there are several statistical problems in obtaining this measure.

A vital issue is the poverty level of wealth today that would correspond to the level of a century ago. The level of $100 chosen for the census figures should be adjusted upward to correct for price changes and probably also for general productivity increases. Prices in 1963 were 3.5 times those in 1860 and 2.5 times those in 1870. If wealth productivity in an age class increased 1.0 percent a year from 1860 to 1963 and prices rose as stated, $100 in 1860 would be $1,000 in 1963. A level of $100 in 1870, coupled with the price increase and productivity increases of 1.5 percent a year, gives $1,000 in 1963. Perhaps this range of productivity increases is not an unreasonable measure of general betterment in the economy.[38] The $100 represented about 4 percent of average wealth in 1860-70, and the $1,000 represented 5 percent of average wealth in 1962-63; they are comparable relative levels.

Table 2.7 gives an accounting of the proportion who were poor (1 − TEH) for selected years. Twenty-five percent of families and unrelated individuals had less than $1,000 in 1962-63—not much more than half the 43 percent who

Table 2.7. Proportion of Adult Males with Total Estate Less Than
$100 in 1860 and 1870 and Families with Less Than
$1,000 in Wealth in 1962-63

	Poor			Nonpoor (TEH)		
Age	1860 nonslaves	1870 all	1962-63	1860 nonslaves	1870 all	1962-63
Under 35	.53	.59	.49	.47	.41	.51
35-54	.24	.31	.20	.76	.69	.80
55-64	.19	.24	.15	.81	.76	.85
65 and up	.29	.30	.18	.71	.70	.82
All	.38	.43	.25	.62	.57	.75

Source: See table 2.6.

were poor in 1870. A major explanation in the 18 percent
decrease, however, is the aging of the population. The difference is almost exactly 10 percent for individuals in each
specific age group listed in the table. It is noted for the four
age classes that the differences are 10, 11, 9, and 12 percentage points. One can say that the poverty configurations
for 1 – TEH and age are parallel for the two years, with one
curve lying below the other by a distance representing 10
percent of the population of each age group. The improvement is certainly significant for the century, and for the age
group 55-64 it means that the poor have been cut from 24
to 15 persons per 100.

One might maintain that 1 – TEH has not dropped very
much for a country that has been proud of its growth. The
difference for 1870 and 1962-63 is .35 – .25 if we standardize for age by using the 1962-63 population of age classes
as weights. The poverty group has decreased only 10/35,
or one-third of the maximum that it might have. One-fourth
of the country's people are poor rather than the just over
one-third of a century earlier. It is not possible to state
exactly when this improvement occurred during the century,
but if the data on homeownership are a guide, it is likely to
have taken place largely since World War II.

The Poor among Negroes

Some mention should be made of the record of Negroes before and after the Civil War in achieving property and minimum wealth accumulation. A small sample of 151 free colored was obtained from the 1850 spin sample. Their average age was similar to that of whites but they were much more predominantly in the rural sector (95 percent were farmers). By limiting detail to age classes above and below 40 years of age, we find the differences for PH between the two groups in the accompanying table.

Age	PH of free colored in 1850	PH of all free in 1850
20-39	.06	.31
40-99	.16	.60
All	.10	.41

The probability of a free colored male's owning property was very small indeed, about one-fourth of that of all freemen in 1850.

The sample size of 1,096 nonwhites in 1870 is much larger. In the accompanying table I consider color of skin in relation to our usual variables.

Color	Population proportion	Average age	Farmer proportion	PH	TEH
Mulattoes	.09	35	.62	.11	.25
Blacks	.91	37	.69	.05	.18
All non-whites	1.00	36	.68	.06	.19

Propertyholder probability was twice as high for mulattoes as for blacks. One might suppose that there would be little semblance of an age parabola in this initial census year after freedom from slavery. However, there was a gradient with a PH of .05 for those under 40 and .08 for those over 40. There is no doubt that few nonwhites held property.

Total estate holdings reflect ownership of personal estate; a rather surprising 19 percent of nonwhites held wealth in

1870. The small number living in the North had a TEH of
.33, as opposed to one of .18 for those living in the South.
Classification by age is given in the accompanying table.

Age	TEH of nonwhites	TEH of whites
20-39	.16	.51
40-99	.25	.76

The absolute difference in proportions is less among the
young than among the old. This is evidence of the initial
climb of nonwhites in closing the gap between the groups.

The effect of color on the relative number of poor is more
dramatically illustrated when southern and northern experiences are contrasted. There was only a slight increase in
the proportion of poor (1 - TEH) among white southerners
from 1860 to 1870. The record was still better for whites
in the South than in the North in 1870, largely because
there were relatively more farmers in the former. It is only
when nonwhites are added to the picture in 1870 that the
advantage swings clearly to the North. In that year, 50 of
every 100 in the South were poor while 40 of every 100 in
the North were poor. The figures for farmers in the South
and North were 45 and 25 per 100, respectively, indicating
that there were many fewer poor farmers in the North.

The Poor before 1860

Whether or not the proportion of men without wealth
grew or diminished in the century from the Revolutionary
era to the Civil War is a debatable but significant issue in
terms of participatory democracy. Any long-run trend or
cycle may have existed but we will entertain only three
possibilities: that relative poverty increased, decreased, or
remained constant from 1776 to 1860 or, more specifically,
from 1800 to 1860. The hypothesis that it increased would
be based on the extension of the thesis presented earlier
that society was becoming more urban with greater influxes
of foreign born swelling the populations of cities. The

alternative hypothesis that the proportion without wealth
decreased would rest on the proposition that the mechanism
for land settlement was improved and that more fertile lands
became available. One having the latter view would be strongly influenced by what he perceived to occur in Ohio, Kentucky, and Mississippi after 1800 or 1810 with the improvement in transportation and communication. According to
the second hypothesis those without property in the period
from 1820 to 1840 could move with increasing ease to relatively abundant supplies of productive land. The productivity
of the farms would allow a surplus above necessary consumption and the accumulation of wealth.

One can find contemporary writers on both sides of this
issue. Those living in eastern cities could observe the ingress
of the poor and also the egress of ordinary people to the
West.[39] There is yet a third hypothesis that the proportion
who were poor remained essentially constant, at least after
1800. This stems mostly from the finding of constancy after
the Civil War, but it is also based on the proposition that immigration into the United States and to the West proceeded
only at a pace allowing constant probability of hardship. If
conditions were severe or were becoming severe, signals appeared in the settled regions or in Europe that curtailed in-
flows.

The measured poor for 1860 have been designated quite
precisely as $1 - TEH$, or the proportion of adult males with
total estate of less than $100. It is doubtful that there are
comparable figures for an earlier census year. A very strong
inference exists that the proportion was almost the same in
1850 since the propertyholder data of $1 - PH$ were similar
in the two years. Little precise information is available prior
to 1850 except for local tax records, wills, estates, and
probates.

The only scientific count of all poor for a state known by
the author is for Kentucky in 1800. Each individual 21 and
older was required to declare ownership of farm acreage,

town lots, slaves, horses, carriages, stores, and taverns
throughout the state for the purpose of state property
taxation, including a poll tax. The total number of men
corresponds remarkably well with that reported by the
Federal Census of 1800. I drew a sample of 980 men from
the records and, with an adjustment for those of age 20,
determined that 81 percent of men had wealth.[40] The spin
sample for Kentucky in 1860 reported 79 percent with
wealth. Thus the proportion who were poor in this agricultural state was the *same* at the beginning and at the end of
a 60-year period. There probably was a dominant form of
agricultural production that evolved in a regular and consistent fashion. This likelihood is illustrated by the fact
that there were 22 slaveholders per 100 free adult males in
the state in 1800 and 1850, and 18 per 100 in 1860.

The only other piece of information available pertains to
slaveholders, a limited group of affluent individuals. A
southerner who was not a slaveholder certainly could not
be considered poor but we might examine the data as indicators of stability or instability of upper wealth groups. I
estimate that slaveholders constituted 27 percent of southern adult men in 1830, 23 percent in 1850, and 19 percent
in 1860. The number of slaveholders per family I estimate
to have been .36 in 1790, .36 in 1830, .31 in 1850, and
.25 in 1860.[41] The figures are influenced by an important
rural–urban movement in the South and by the fact that
the number of families increased more rapidly than did
slaves. The ratios, at the least, depict an absence of cyclical
movement.

The only other clues stem from our age classifications for
native born in 1850 and 1860. An individual who entered
the labor force at age 20 is included in our statistics if he
lived to the age of 70. The data confirm that his experience
was similar to that of those 10 years younger than himself.
The PH–age parabola for those 60 and older was consistent
after 1850 so we have no reason to believe that the poverty

experience of one entering the labor force in 1800 was any
different from that of one entering at a later date. Consider
the accompanying table for PH ratios for native born as an
example of consistency.

	Age 60-69	Age 70-79
1850	.69	.60
1860	.72	.60

The reason our age parabolas are so important is that they
convey past history. Wealth positions, not nearly so transient
as income positions, are more likely to be a record of sustained ability to have positive saving for many years.

It is desirable to show that age parabolas existed in 1800
and were similar to those of 1850 and 1860 if we are to
confirm that there was a stable pattern. This will be accomplished by using census age and slave data for households in
1800 and personal estate data for 1860. They yield similar
age parabolas.[42] (Appendix table A 3 gives proportions holding personal estates of $100 or more.) The data are presented
in the accompanying table.

Age class	Proportion of slaveholders in 1800 in five slave areas	Proportion of men in the South in 1860 with personal estate of	
		$500 or more	$600 or more
20-25	.15	.14	.12
26-44	.33	.38	.30
45 and up	.44	.50	.44
20 and up	.32	.35	.30

I studied the personal estate data for 1860 to the point where
the proportion of men with personal estate was equivalent
to the slaveholder proportion in 1800 (.32). This equivalence
was found to be between $500 and $600. The age parabolas
at these levels were then found to have shapes very sug-
gestive of the 1800 slaveholder–age parabola. Such data support the argument that the configuration did exist in 1800
if poor are defined as those in the South with no slaves. This

standard for the poor of one minus the slaveholder proportion is probably indicative of 1 - TEH.

In New York in 1800 the number of households with
slaves was 6.7 percent of the estimated number of males 20
and older. The accompanying table shows age classifications
for a sample of 787 slaveholders that were obtained by
sampling every tenth household with slaves.

Age class	Proportions of slaveholders in 1800 in New York	Proportion of men in New York in 1860 with personal estate of	
		$2,000 or more	$2,100 or more
20-25	.014	.007	.003
26-44	.060	.077	.058
45 and up	.120	.125	.101
20 and up	.067	.076	.058

If one assumes that all rich, or many rich without age bias,
held slaves in 1800, we are able to look at the percentage of
rich in 1860, who are above the admittedly puzzling value
of $2,000 or $2,100 instead of above $500. This finding
undoubtedly occurs because not all rich were slaveholders
and slaves were more likely to bring higher prices than field
hands in the South. The effect in 1860 is more pervasive
than New York residence. Similar results were found for
1860 for all males *born* in New York and New Jersey. In
any case there is some semblance of similarity in holder
proportions in the North and South in 1800 and 1860.

The available evidence indicates that one should accept
the hypothesis that the proportion who were poor in the
United States remained essentially constant from 1790 to
1860. This acceptance is based on data for PH-age parabolas
for the United States in 1850 and 1860, Kentucky poor in
1800 and 1860, nonslaveholders in the South from 1790 to
1860, and slaveholder-age parabolas in 1800 and 1860.
There is just no evidence of any discontinuities or even of
any unreasonable changes for the data that are available. It
seems that the United States always offered free men the

same opportunity to own property or wealth prior to the
Civil War.

Summary

We have studied in this chapter the proportion of adult
males who were holders of real estate or property (PH), personal estate (PEH), and total estate (TEH). The holder proportions are presented in the accompanying table.

	1850 *nonslaves*	*1860* *nonslaves*	*1870* *whites*	*1870* *all*
PH	.41	.43	.43	.39
PEH	—	.58	.57	.53
TEH	—	.62	.62	.57

These figures exhibit strong constancy even though the
population of adult males increased approximately 40 percent in the first decade and 25 percent (excluding nonwhites) in the second decade. The proportion of nonholders
in the middle of the last century is rather shocking. Well
over one-half were propertyless in the sense that they owned
no land or buildings; well over one-third did not have wealth
of $100 or more.

A study of participation rates by age group exhibits a very
strong and pervasive parabolic effect. Both PH and TEH are
near zero at age 20; they then rise rapidly from 20 to 29,
less rapidly from 30 to 39, and approach maxima at about
age 60. The shapes of these curves imply that the number
of poor obtaining property in a year is about the same as
the increase in the adult population in a year. The parabolas
do remain remarkably the same for 1850-70. A study of
nativity and age reveals that one-half of America's poor were
foreign born living in urban areas. The probability of ownership was 15-25 percent higher if one lived in a farm area
rather than in an urban area and 5-10 percent higher if one
was native born rather than foreign born.

The differences in farm and nonfarm values of PH lead to

the suggestion that studies by region of residence would be fruitful. PH rose substantially in proceeding from East to Middle West in a given year. There is evidence that an initial increase in PH occurred in an area in earlier stages of land settlement and then a drop as more marginal land was encountered and nonfarm development took place. In my study of individuals by region or country of birth, the gamut of PH for men classified by country of birth was Ireland, with a rate one-half that of native born, followed by Germany and then Britain. I found that northeasterners who moved west had the same PH and TEH levels as those remaining in the Northeast.

A projection of PH to 1960 was made on the basis of 1870 data on PH for age, occupation, and nativity classes and of the populations of these classes in each decade to 1960. I found that the urban movement would bring a decrease in PH but that this drop would be counterbalanced by the decrease in numbers of foreign born and, even more importantly, by the increase in average age. Data on home-ownership after 1890 provide some verification of the projection. A careful comparison of the proportion of people without wealth (1 - TEH) demonstrates that 43 percent of men had wealth of less than $100 in 1870 and 25 percent had less wealth than its corresponding dollar minimum in 1962-63. Half this difference can be explained by aging, so there are about 10 percent fewer poor today than a century ago with newly enfranchised Negroes. An analysis of early statistical data concludes that the proportion who were poor remained the same from 1800 to 1860.

There are two very general conclusions concerning the proportion of men holding wealth in the United States. Patterns for nonslaves in 1850 and 1860 and for whites in 1870 were remarkably stable. The most striking finding was that this country harbored vast proportions of populations with no wealth.

3. The Average Value of Real and Total Estate

This chapter surveys the mean wealth level of men from the three censuses in our study by considering, first, the strong gains in the decade before the war and, second, the losses in the South and the constancy in the North in the decade encompassing the Civil War. The comparisons are somewhat cumbersome to handle because adjustments must be made both for slave values and for inflation. Next, I relate mean wealth to our standard variables of age, occupation, nativity, and residence in determining what an individual could have expected to gain during his lifetime. This is followed by three sections that place the study means in a wider perspective. One section focuses on various estimates of wealth means since 1800; another section is devoted to a limited time model encompassing births, deaths, and inheritance; and the final section deals with the relationship among mean wealth, annual saving, and income.

The motives and experiences of men are so diverse that there is a danger in describing the amorphous average man. In the field of wealth accumulation one surely should distinguish between the poor and rich; yet each may be subject to the spirit and mores of the entire economic society. Francis Bowen argued thus in 1856 when he wrote: "The most striking thing in the aspect of society here is the constant strain of the faculties, in all classes, in the pursuit of wealth,—the restlessness, the feverish anxiety to get on."[1] Herman Melville wrote more poignantly in 1854 about how the ideas of universal equality pervaded the lives of all classes.

> The native American poor never lose their delicacy or pride; hence, though unreduced to the physical degradation of the European pauper, they yet suffer more in mind than the poor of any other people in the world.

> Those peculiar social sensibilities nourished by our own
> political principles, while they enhance the true dignity
> of a prosperous American, do but minister to the added
> wretchedness of the unfortunate.[2]

The statistics on wealth averages presented in this chapter
are generalizations of success and failure that do represent
the economic adventure of a wide spectrum of men at midcentury.

Mean Real Estate

The arithmetic mean of real estate holdings was $1,001 for
the 5.0 million free men in 1850 ($\overline{RE}$ = $1,001). This very
substantial figure was the equivalent of roughly $4,000 in
terms of 1970 prices.[3] It should be emphasized, however,
that not everyone held this mean wealth. At one extreme
there were millionaires, and at the other, the propertyless;
yet only about one-fifth of free men owned more than the
average. If one overlooks the problem of distribution, he
could justifiably be proud of this exceptionally high figure.
It was high relative to wealthholdings today. If the $1,001
were to grow at an annual rate of 1.5 percent a year, it could
account for the average wealth of families in 1962-63. Or,
if it were to grow at an annual rate of only 1.1 percent a
year, it could account for the average value of real estate
today.[4] But the distribution is such that 4 of every 10
families today do not have real estate that matches $\overline{RE}$ in
1850.[5]

The average does not seem so large relative to the level of
income in 1850. We obtain a real estate/income ratio of
$1,001/$399 = 2.5 by using an estimate of Simon Kuznets's.[6]
This ratio rises to 3.1/1 if an adjustment is made to yield
total estate.[7] An estimate will be presented later for average
total estate of $1,223 in 1850 after adjusting for slavery. Is
a wealth/income ratio of 3 large or small? At least one

prominent economist of the period made an amazing estimate in the 1860s of this ratio and found it to be 3.7.[8] He was surprised that it was not greater than it was because he was so impressed by the power of saving with compound interest. Presumably he thought that the ratio might be 5/1 or more in a dynamic economy. It was more likely to have been that level in less dynamic circumstances. At the time several European countries had ratios of 5/1 or more.[9] Land and other natural resources played a more prominent part in the generation of income in these countries than was the case in the United States. The fact that income from assets was a larger part of total income contributed to the greater relative inequality existing abroad.[10]

The average value of real estate grew from $1,001 in 1850 to $1,492 in 1860 and to $1,782 for whites in 1870. This gives a change, in current dollars, of 49 percent in the first decade and of 19 percent in the second. The consumer price index climbed from 90 to 100 to 141 in the three years; the real growth of the first decade is reduced to 34 percent and that of the second to a loss of 15 percent. The loss from 1860 to 1870 arose largely in the South, which suffered a decline in $\overline{RE}$ of 45 percent in real terms. The northern $\overline{RE}$, as determined from our spin samples and corrected for price changes, was the *same* before and after the war.

It is true that the mythical average northern man in 1860 had the same real estate as did his counterpart in 1870. But the two are different men; within the composite some would have died and others would have appeared. We shall see later that most specific age cohorts had real gains in real estate as they grew 10 years older in the Civil War decade. There is even a little evidence that real gains would have been the same in both decades if there had been no inflation. One could draw such an inference from the fact that northern $\overline{RE}$ increased by the same percentage in both decades, as measured in current dollars, and that this held true for the averages of various age classes. Inflation may have wiped out the effect of the sustained growth that might otherwise have arisen from age patterns as men progressed from their twenties in 1850 to their thirties in 1860 and to their forties in 1870.

Mean Total Estate

The arithmetic mean of total estate of adult males ($\overline{\overline{TE}}$) is a difficult concept to discuss in making comparisons between the periods before and after the Civil War. One confounding problem is that for the prewar South, only free men reported total estate, which includes the value of slaves in personal estate. The computed average wealth for 1860 is greater than it otherwise would be because the numerator includes slave values and the denominator does not include adult males who were slaves. Points of difference can be found in table 3.1.

Table 3.1. Average Wealth ($\overline{\overline{TE}}$) for Adult Males by Residence

	1860 *free*	*1870* *whites*	*1870* *all*
United States	$2,580	$2,691(1,910)	$2,399(1,700)
North	2,040	2,921(2,070)	2,884(2,040)
South	3,978	2,034(1,440)	1,428(1,010)

Sources: Spin samples of 13,696 and 9,823 from schedules 1 of the 1860 and 1870 censuses, respectively.

Note: Averages adjusted to 1860 prices are given in parentheses.

The $\overline{\overline{TE}}$ of $2,040 for the North is derived from aggregate valuation, two-thirds of which was in real estate and one-third in personal estate. The real estate value was in farmland, lots, houses, and buildings; the personal estate was in bonds, stocks, mortgages, notes, livestock, jewels, and furniture. During the decade the northern average grew 41 percent, the same increase as the rate of inflation. The record indicates that those in the Northwest fared better than those in Northeast in this period, which was marked by very high rates of taxation and war financing.

The situation in the South is much more difficult to describe with statistical averages. One observes first from table 3.1 that the $\overline{\text{TE}}$ of southern free men in 1860 was almost twice as large as that in the North. The $1,900 advantage could be attributed to the fact that there were 2.0 slaves per white adult male in the South. A study to be presented in chapter 4 establishes that slaves were valued, on the average, at about $900 each in the 1860 census. The wealth of southern *whites* dropped from an average of about $4,000 in 1860 to a real value little more than one-third of this amount in 1870. It would take 50-100 years for the southern white average to rise again to a real value of $4,000, assuming that long-run per capita growth in real wealth is 1-2 percent a year. By 1870 the $\overline{\text{TE}}$ for southern whites had fallen to abou two-thirds that in the North. Therefore, whites in the South went from a twice to a two-thirds position in wealth relative to men in the North. Not all this change could be explained by the loss of slaves, because real estate values also declined. The $\overline{\text{RE/TE}}$ ratio for whites in the South dropped by 1870 to the same figure that existed for the North.

The southern position must be elaborated further in adjusting to the concept of a free population in 1870. The average wealth of all persons was two-thirds of the southern white value essentially because there was one nonwhite for every two whites among adult males. This strange inversion of wealth averages was brought about by emancipation. In the country of free men in 1860 average wealth was twice as large in the South as in the North. In the country of free men in 1870 average wealth in the North was twice as large as in the South.

Wealth Averages Adjusted for Slaves

A more thorough calculation of growth would adjust both the aggregate wealth and aggregate population in 1860 to a nonslave basis. The resulting average, $\overline{\text{TE}}_{\text{slave adj, 1860}}$, can

then be compared to $\overline{TE}_{all, 1870}$. The estimate is based on
table 5.4, which shows the average value of slaves was $900,
as reported in the 1860 census. The numerator of each average is reduced by $900 times the number of slaves, and the
denominator is increased to include the number of adult
male slaves. This calculation is repugnant in the sense that
freedom means more than dollars. I add an estimate in table
3.2[11] for 1850 based on the real estate aggregate in that year
and on the importance of real estate in 1860.

Table 3.2. Mean Total Estate Adjusted for Slaves ($\overline{TE}_{slave\ adj}$) of All
Adult Males, 1850-70

	$\overline{TE}_{slave\ adj,\ 1850}$	$\overline{TE}_{slave\ adj,\ 1860}$	$\overline{TE}_{1870}$
United States	$1,223(1,350)	$1,853	$2,399(1,700)
North	1,463(1,620)	2,040	2,884(2,040)
South	850(940)	1,521	1,428(1,010)

Source: See table 3.1 and the text (n. 11).

Note: Averages in 1860 dollars are given in parentheses.

The average annual percentage of change for 1850-1860,
1860-1870, and 1850-1870 in the United States was 4.2, 2.6,
and 3.4, respectively, in current dollars and 3.1, -0.9, and
1.1 in constant dollars. There was a real loss in wealth in the
Civil War decade. Professor Kuznets's percentages for gross
national product per worker for these three periods are 1.7,
-0.1, and .8 in constant dollars. Those of Robert Gallman for
commodity output per worker are 2.1, 0.2, and 1.2 in constant dollars.[12] There is a strong parallel between changes in
wealth and income in the United States.

The separate wealth estimate for the North leads to percentage growth rates of 2.3, 0.0, and 1.2, respectively, for
1850-60, 1860-70, and 1850-70. (These rates are remarkably close to Gallman's income figures for the United States.)
Those for southern wealth are 4.9, -4.0, and 0.3. Perhaps
southern wealth for all men in 1870 was like that in 1850,
equivalent to a 20-year loss.

It is noted that $\overline{TE}_{all, South}/\overline{TE}_{all, North}$ was .58, .75, and .50 in 1850, 1860, and 1870. The figures reflect a stronger economic position of the South relative to the North in 1860 than in 1850 (based on real estate figures). But never was the system in the South so strong as that in the North from the standpoint of wealth per human being. For wealth in the South, $\overline{TE}_{all}$ in 1870 was two-thirds of that in 1860 when expressed in real dollars. If growth were 1-2 percent a year, the South suffered 30 or more years' loss from its 1860 level. This is an overstatement, not only because the catch-up rate after 1870 might be more rapid, but also because the previous slave economy could not be sustained.

Land and slave values, which played a very important part in the valuation of wealth from 1850 to 1870, will be discussed at length in succeeding sections. The part of wealth-holdings produced by men in the form of structures, equipment, and durable goods of consumers has been studied extensively by Raymond Goldsmith. His estimates of the composition of the reproducible tangible wealth aggregate in the United States in 1850 convey the details of the quantitative significance of these assets. Nonfarm consumers held 24 percent of the total value (19 percent in residences and 5 percent in consumer durable goods); farmers held 38 percent (half in structures and equipment and half in livestock, crops, and consumer goods); nonagricultural business constituted 38 percent (27 percent in structures and 11 percent in inventories); governmental and international components were small. Thus, structures of all types constituted more than half of the wealth made by man. Consumer durable goods such as furniture and jewelry, the articles sometimes displayed in museums today, were but a small part of the total. Estimates for 1880 indicate that the relative importance of reproducible tangible wealth in the farm sector decreased dramatically after 1850.[13] This analysis does not include the value of land, which is a vital aspect of the wealth of individuals. One extrapolation of Goldsmith's data from 1900 to 1950 yields an estimate that aggregate land value may have been as much as 80 percent of aggregate reproducible tangible wealth in 1850.[14]

Age

It was understandable that wealth and age should be positively related at midcentury because material betterment dominated the economic thinking of men. Those with wealth expected to have more each year as they grew older; accumulation was a sign or an index of recognition of an individual's past economic activities. Wealth mirrors the past better than income since the pleasures of past consumption may be forgotten. It is only the saving from past income that is now reflected in one's wealth. Bowen expressed this idea in 1856 when he stated:

> Every individual here has the power to make savings, if he will, and almost as large as he will,—and has the certainty that the savings when made, the wealth when accumulated, will immediately operate, in proportion to its amount, to raise the frugal person's position in life,—to give him, in fact, the only distinction that is recognized among us.[15]

An individual might work as hard, or harder, in the United States than he would have worked in another country as long as he could see real growth of his wealth. It is not trite to repeat some maxims of the time. Freeman Hunt wrote in *Worth and Wealth* (1856): "Time is gold. . . . Deprive yourself of nothing necessary to your comfort but live in honorable simplicity and frugality. Labor then to the last moment of your existence." The model was one of steps on a staircase or ladder. An individual was supposed to rise "until he stands securely at the summit, with fame, wealth and honors surrounding him." The summit was reached by "faith,

industry, perseverence, temperance, probity, and inde-
pendence . . . and not by luck, scheming, or patronage."[16]

Realholders

The Census of 1850 records man's material achievement
in real estate holdings at various age levels. These census
statistics for a whole country may be unique in the world
from the standpoint of being the earliest recording of a
comprehensive measure of economic achievement at various
age levels of the population.[17] The mean value of real estate
in the United States climbed steadily for those 20 and older,
as shown by chart 3.1 and the accompanying table.

Age	$\overline{RE}_{age}$	Incremental increase, $\triangle \overline{RE}_{age}$
20-29	$ 253	
30-39	835	$582
40-49	1,639	804
50-59	1,950	311
60-69	2,253	303
70-99	2,439	186

The group average rises strongly from 20-29 to 30-39 and
then has its greatest thrust in going from the 30-39 to the
40-49 group. The average tapers off but continues to rise
rather surprisingly into old age. There is certainly no strong
parabolic effect, as can be seen in chart 3.1. One recalls
from the preceding chapter that the proportion of men
with property showed a strong parabolic effect when
plotted for age groups. This phenomenon occurred principally before age 40 however, and the rapid increase in the
relative number having property is partly responsible for
the strong increase in the $\overline{RE}$ curve before age 40.

The difference in wealth levels from one year to the next
gives an index of saving for a year. It appears that the
greatest saving is for the age group in their late thirties and
early forties but saving appears to continue even into old

Chart 3.1. Mean Value of Real Estate ($\overline{\text{RE}}$) and Total Estate ($\overline{\text{TE}}$) of Adult Free Males, 1850-70

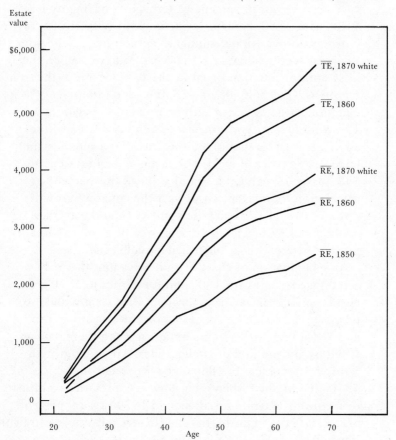

Sources: Spin samples.

age. The average increase is about $500 for each decade group from 20 to 59 or 20 to 69, a span covering well over 90 percent of adult males. Wealth rises about $2,500 in 50 years of adult life, or roughly $50 a year as estimated from the 1850 data. This initial estimate of annual saving (s = $\overline{\Delta RE}$) can be put in percentage terms by dividing by $\overline{RE}$ = $1,001 for 1850. Perhaps saving is about $50/$1,001, or 5 percent of wealth per annum as determined solely from the cross-sectional data for that year. More formally, the least-squares equation fitted to all 10,393 items in the spin sample is RE = $52.50(age – 18.0) = $\overline{\Delta RE}$ (adult age).[18] The equation suggests that wealth accumulation begins at age 18 and is *directly proportional to adult age.* One whose adult age is twice that of another has an expected accumulated saving twice as large. The saving in real estate is $52.50, or 5.2 percent a year. I will call this percentage calculation for a given census year the apparent growth rate, AGR = $\overline{\Delta RE}/\overline{RE}$. Those younger than the average adult age of 37 had an increase in wealth greater than 5.2 percent whereas those older had a smaller increase.

An examination of chart 3.1 indicates that the real estate–age patterns for 1860 and for whites in 1870 are also essentially linear. They begin at zero wealth and are proportional to adult age. Slopes of $68 a year for 1860 and $84 a year for 1870 are obtained when these data are fitted by the method of straight lines. Apparent growth rates of 4.6 percent in 1860 and 4.7 percent for whites in 1870 are obtained when each slope is expressed as a ratio of its mean. The rate for all men in 1870 was 4.9 percent.

The statistics indicate that the $\overline{RE}$–age pattern is a straight line, with the slope $\overline{\Delta RE}$ becoming steeper each year as economic growth proceeds. The slope of each line at mid-century was about 5 percent of average wealth. It can be shown mathematically that the apparent growth rate is equal to the reciprocal of adult age, that is, AGR = 1/(adult age) = 1/(age – K), where K is 16 to 18 years of age. Thus,

AGR varied from about $1/(37-18) = .053$ to perhaps $1/(38-17) = .047$ at midcentury.

Age and Time Betterment

Chart 3.1 demonstrates that the individual experiences two effects through time, an age effect and a general time effect. For example, a man moves from a position at age 30 in 1850 to a position at 40 on the 1860 curve. The relative movement from age 30 to 40 is the age effect as measured by the apparent growth rate, AGR. The movement from one curve to the next, which arises because of economic growth, is called the general growth rate, GGR. This latter growth has been measured as somewhere between 1.0 and 2.0 percent a year. The estimate of expected increase for the individual in midcentury was AGR + GGR of about $.05 + .02$, or 7.0 percent a year as a maximum, or perhaps $.046 + .010$, or 5.6 percent as a minimum. A possible equation for the expected wealth of an individual of given adult age in year t is $RE_{age,t} = \$50(\text{adult age})(1.015)^{t-1850}$. It captures the two effects, improvement with age and improvement of general economic conditions.[19]

The apparent growth effect is clearly dominant from the standpoint of the individual. It transcends any cyclical activity that may slow the general trend. The decade of the Civil War is a case in point since there was no real shift in our linear pattern, that is, the general growth rate, GGR, was zero. The individual still could proceed generally along the $\overline{RE}$-age path at an average rate of about 5 percent a year if he were of average age.

There is some implication that the individual dissaves after he is in his forties because the interest rate was about 5 percent while his accumulation rate on wealth was less than 5 percent. Consider the statement "The first half-eagle which the laboring man or woman saves from the month's wages is profitably invested, and, by the end of the year, is

increased by the twentieth part of itself."[20] This is true only
if he does not spend his 5 percent interest. It is important to
realize that the $\overline{\text{RE}}$–age curve does not grow geometrically
with age. Decreased vigor might lower labor income and
increase investment conservatism. This would necessitate
increasing use of consumption spending from earnings on
estate investment. The $\overline{\text{RE}}$–age path is, at best, one that increases by constant amounts each year.

Wealthholders

The evidence obtained from working with *total* estate
averages, classified by the age of men, is that there is again
a linear relationship. Examination of the $\overline{\text{TE}}$–age lines for
1860 and 1870 presented in chart 3.1 indicates a slight
curvilinear effect but such wealth essentially is proportional
to adult age: a person in the labor force three times as long
as another had three times as much wealth.

The apparent growth rates, calculated from least-squares
equations, are .044 in 1860, .045 for whites in 1870, and
.047 for all in 1870. The rate of .046 in the North in 1870
is fairly consistent for all occupation and nativity groups.
It is reasonable to use an AGR of .045 in dealing with the
wealth of individuals. The AGR is vitally important as our
measure of betterment for the individual. At any point in
time the average man had wealth 4.5 percent greater than
that of a man one year younger. This, coupled with economic growth of perhaps 1.5 percent, would mean that the
individual had 6 percent more wealth in one year than he
had in the preceding year.

The individual shared in two improvement factors, as
manifested in the line representing age differences at a point
in time and the shift in this line through time. These strong
effects meant that wealth accumulation must have been a
dominating influence in America. The stability of the pattern found for 1850 is proof that the age patterns were

established decades before 1850 and that the concepts of economic betterment must have been pervasive. Tocqueville wrote in the 1830s:

> In America, every one finds facilities unknown else-
> where for making or increasing his fortune. The spirit of
> gain is always on the stretch, and the human mind,
> constantly diverted from the pleasures of imagination
> and the labors of the intellect, is there swayed by no
> impulse but the pursuit of wealth.[21]

Such was the harsh criticism of a French aristocrat as he observed the United States less than a score of years before our statistical recordings of 1850.

Occupation

It is certainly to be expected that the average real estate of farmers would be substantially more than that of nonfarmers. One notes in table 3.3 that it was twice as large in 1850 and 1.7 times as large in 1860 for free men. The depressed agricultural conditions in the South and proper accounting for nonwhites in 1870 meant that mean real estate was only 30 percent greater for farmers than nonfarmers! Even in this case part of the difference can be explained by the fact that nonfarmers were younger than farmers. For those 40 and older, mean real estate of farmers was only 14 percent larger than for nonfarmers.

The value of some urban real estate was substantial enough in 1870 to compensate for the fact that the proportion of men holding property was half again as high in rural areas as it was in urban areas. As far as aggregate value of real estate in 1870 was concerned, farmers held 55 percent and non-farmers 45 percent. The population in the nonfarm sector was growing rapidly, and increases in the value of urban lots, if not of homes and buildings, were due in part to capital gains.

Table 3.3. Mean Value of Real Estate ($\overline{RE}$) of Adult Males in the
            United States in 1850, 1860, and 1870 by Nativity and
            Occupation

	1850 free	1860 free	1870 whites	1870 all
All persons	$1,001	$1,492	$1,783	$1,587
Native born	1,103	1,722	2,001	1,714
Foreign born	535	833	1,215	1,204
Farmers[a]	1,385	1,894	2,141	1,808
Native born	1,401	2,035	2,143	1,762
Foreign born	1,195	1,187	2,134	2,121
Nonfarmers[a]	694	1,099	1,480	1,382
Native born	805	1,328	1,836	1,654
Foreign born	380	669	911	902

Sources: Spin samples of 10,393; 13,696; and 9,823 from schedules
1 of the 1850, 1860, and 1870 censuses.

[a]In 1850 farm laborers generally were not classified as farmers.

It is when one turns to total estate, or real plus personal
estate, that he can establish clearly that the balance shifted
in favor of the urban sector. The farm mean value in 1860
was 50 percent larger than the nonfarm mean but the differential was smaller among the old, as shown in table 3.4.
For whites in 1870, the farm mean was 19 percent higher
for all adults 20 and older, whereas nonfarmers had the advantage in the age group over 40 (see chart 3.2). For whites
and nonwhites in the United States in 1870, mean total
estate was 8 percent larger for farmers, but nonfarmers had
the advantage after age 40.

Nativity

The ratio of the mean real estate of native born to foreign
born ($\overline{RE}_{NB}/\overline{RE}_{FB}$) was 2.0 in 1850 and in 1860, and 1.7
for whites in 1870. Table 3.3 shows this differential to have
been mainly in the urban sector, where the ratio remained
essentially 2.0 for all three study years. There was dramatic

Table 3.4. Mean Value of Total Estate ($\overline{TE}$) of Adult Males in the
United States in 1860 and 1870 by Age, Nativity, and
Occupation

	Age			
	20-99	*20-29*	*30-39*	*40-99*
		1860 free		
All persons	$2,580	$ 886	$1,999	$4,543
Native born	3,027	979	2,444	5,264
Foreign born	1,297	592	1,051	2,188
Farmers	3,166	1,109	2,489	5,083
Native born	3,453	1,174	2,753	5,562
Foreign born	1,720	717	1,473	2,571
Nonfarmers	2,006	700	1,601	3,850
Native born	2,492	772	2,106	4,785
Foreign born	1,099	544	879	1,950
		1870 whites		
All persons	$2,691	$ 701	$2,110	$4,602
Native born	3,035	807	2,363	5,323
Foreign born	1,798	341	1,578	2,844
Farmers	2,948	955	2,538	4,488
Native born	2,974	984	2,510	4,662
Foreign born	2,800	693	2,674	3,673
Nonfarmers	2,475	510	1,802	4,716
Native born	3,106	630	2,209	6,254
Foreign born	1,468	260	1,267	2,484
		1870 all		
All persons	$2,399	$ 614	$1,897	$4,146
Native born	2,604	683	2,034	4,622
Foreign born	1,783	338	1,563	2,820
Farmers	2,494	780	2,144	3,900
Native born	2,451	788	2,057	3,945
Foreign born	2,783	687	2,656	3,650
Nonfarmers	2,311	472	1,698	4,415
Native born	2,798	566	2,007	5,640
Foreign born	1,454	257	1,254	2,461

Sources: Spin samples of 13,696 and 9,823 from schedules 1 of the
1860 and 1870 censuses, respectively.

improvement in the ratio for foreign-born farmers by 1870,
principally due to deteriorated conditions in the South.

Chart 3.2. Mean Value of Total Estate by Nativity, Age, and Occupation for White Males in 1870

Mean total
estate, $\overline{TE}$

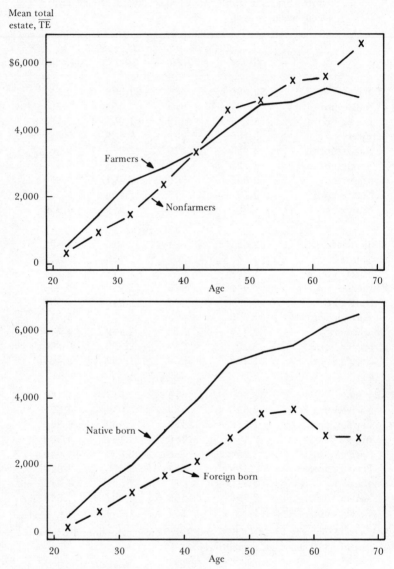

Sources: Spin samples.

Note: Means are unweighted averages of three points in a 15-year period.

However, the degree of improvement found for the North was partly a result of curtailed immigration rates during the war.

The mean wealth ratio $(\overline{TE}_{NB}/\overline{TE}_{FB})$ was very large in urban areas (2.3 in 1860 and 2.1 in 1870). The size of this urban disparity is all the more poignant if one considers the fact that there was essentially no disparity in farm areas of the United States by 1870 (see table 3.4). It must be remembered that the percentage of whites who were foreign born was three times as high in the North as in the South. Although the postwar period placed foreign born in a better relative position in the United States farm sector as a whole, a nativity differential still existed in the North among farmers, the $\overline{TE}_{NB}/\overline{TE}_{FB}$ being 1.6 in 1860 and 1.3 in 1870. A further complication arises in attempting to explain general disparity because the foreign-born population was even more urban in 1870 than in 1860. This movement would militate against any relative rise in the status of the foreign born.

I have stressed that the foreign-born handicap was due not only to the language barrier but also to illiteracy. A random sample of 521 illiterate men drawn from the microfilm of the 1860 census revealed a disproportionately large share of foreign-born nonfarmers. The mean wealth of illiterate men was the very low figure of $569, a value but one-fifth of the national average. The wealth average increased from age 20 to 30 but remained constant for those in the age group 30–60. Illiterates participated in a little initial accumulation of wealth and the holding of property but generally were not able to share further in the usual experience of wealth accumulation.

Age, Occupation, Nativity, and Residence

The relationship between the wealth of men and their various socioeconomic characteristics may be generalized by using multiple regression equations. Let us pick just one equation, that for the total estate of all men in the United States in 1870 according to age, occupation, nativity, and residence, and discuss its various regression coefficients:

$$TE_{1870} = -\$960 + \$111 \text{ age} + \$46 \text{ nA} - \$1,421 \text{ FB} - \$1,686 \text{ So},$$

where the average wealth is \$2,399. One observes first that the apparent growth rate with respect to age, AGR, is \$111/\$2,399 = .047. This underlying factor persisted whether or not many variables were considered in an equation. We next note an insignificant advantage of \$46 associated with being a nonfarmer (nA = 1) rather than a farmer (nA = 0) if other variables in the equation are held constant. Remarkably, it means that there was no advantage in being a farmer. The penalty was severe for being foreign born (FB = 1) instead of native born (FB = 0); it was an amount equivalent to 60 percent of average wealth of all persons. Finally, the -\$1,686 coefficient means that the penalty for being a southerner (So = 1) rather than a northerner (So = 0) was even more severe. The southern coefficient would have been about 50 percent of average wealth if we had added another variable for whites and nonwhites.

The above equation form fitted to the data for 1860 non-slaves and 1870 whites may be the best succinct generalization of the change in wealth levels during the Civil War decade.

$$TE_{1860 \text{ free}} = -\$1,059 + \$110 \text{ age} - \$428 \text{ nA} - \$1,211 \text{ FB} + \$1,749 \text{ So}.$$

$$TE_{1870 \text{ white}} = -\$1,380 + \$121 \text{ age} + \$40 \text{ nA} - \$1,535 \text{ FB} - \$1,132 \text{ So}.$$

The coefficient for age shows exceptional stability in AGR terms. That for urbanity changes sign or, at least, indicates that any farm advantage has disappeared.[22] The coefficient for foreign born increased a bit in importance and that for southern residence plummeted.

Westward Migration

Some of the effect of migration may be captured by comparing men in the Northeast and Northwest, which are,
respectively, northern states east and west of the Ohio–
Pennsylvania border. The proportion of northern men in
the Northwest was 1/3 in 1850 and almost 1/2 in 1870—
good evidence of a rapid migration movement. The con-
comitant changes in wealth averages given in table 3.5 indicate that the disparity between the two areas was eliminated

Table 3.5. Mean Real and Total Estate of Adult Men in the Northeast and Northwest, 1850-70

	Real estate		Total estate	
	Northeast	*Northwest*	*Northeast*	*Northwest*
1850	$1,075	$ 832		
1860	1,461	1,284	$2,233	$1,807
1870	1,847	1,948	2,895	2,870

Sources: Spin samples.

in the two decades and that real estate value was actually
higher in the Northwest in 1870. The transformation
occurred because of the differential gains of foreign born
and farmers in the Northwest in 1860-70 relative to their
counterparts in the Northeast.[23] Moreover, the foreign born
in the West had much more real estate than those in the
East. This improvement might not have been so apparent in
1860, since there was a tripling of the foreign-born population and a doubling of the native-born population in the
Northwest from 1850 to 1860. Inefficiencies of land settlement for the newly arrived would have had a greater impact
on the statistics.
    Interesting configurations are found for real estate values
of different age groups within each region. The main finding is that the Northwest in 1850 exhibits *no* RE–age
gradient for those 40 years old and over.[24] This must mean
that these individuals had not been in the region effectively

for more than 20 adult years; they had not experienced long economic growth, in contrast to the pattern of those in the East. Perhaps the configuration can be sketched as in the accompanying chart.

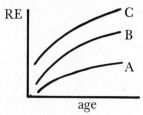

Each additional 10 years of history reveals pattern changes from *A* to *B* and from *A* to *C.* I have studied some counties with only 10 years of history that substantiate this scheme.[25] The issue should not be stressed unduly for 1850, because there were relatively few old males in the West and because the RE–age pattern within the Northwest seemed to be fairly constant whether or not Ohio, Indiana, and Illinois were excluded. The margin-of-settlement and safety-valve theories are better studied at the county level than the state level even in 1850. Roughly speaking, however, settlement states had twice the growth in real estate value per male compared to the already settled states in the period from 1850 to 1860 Right at the frontier there would be great upward shifts over time in the RE–age curves.

Wealth Growth since 1800

General concepts of the magnitude of growth in wealth per person over a long period of time are needed if one is to understand the prevalent shift in the total estate–age curve from decade to decade. The Federal Reserve study for 1962-63 lists average wealth per family at $20,982. If this figure is related to mean total estate in 1870 of $2,399, there is an implicit average annual rate of change of 1.38 percent in real wealth for the 93-year period. If it is related, instead, to the

slave-adjusted estimate of total estate for 1850, there is a
1.34 percent annual change for the 113-year period. Estimates by various authorities usually indicate that growth of
wealth was more rapid in the nineteenth than in the twentieth century. Raymond Goldsmith found that the annual
growth rate of reproducible wealth per head was 2.2 percent
from 1805 to 1850, 2.5 percent from 1850 to 1900, 1.3
percent from 1900 to 1950, or 2.0 percent for the entire
period.[26] John Kendrick has found an average annual rate
of increase in wealth per capita of 1.1 percent in the period
from 1900 to 1967.[27] Horatio Burchard's series shows a
1.8 percent rate between 1825 and 1860.[28] A culling of 30
different estimates of wealth from 1790 to 1963 leads to
a wealth increase estimate of 1.5 percent a year after adjustment for prices and slave values.[29]

There is a method for projecting the farm portion of our
real estate averages from 1850-70 to the present time. The
census bureau has published estimates of the cash value of
farms in the United States from 1850 to 1960. The reported
averages for 1850-70 are almost exactly the same as those
found from the spin samples for farm real estate of farmers
reporting $1 or more of real estate.[30] This finding provides
direct evidence about $\overline{RE}$ after 1870, as given by the plot
of cash value figures presented in chart 3.3. There was a
strong discontinuity between 1860 and 1870 caused by the
plummeting values of southern farms. A trend line fitted to
decennial cash values from 1870 to 1960 shows an average
annual gain of 1.3 percent. The trend from 1870 to 1900
was 1.4 percent a year.

We are in a position to say something more definite about
the two indexes of betterment, namely, the general growth
rate in mean wealth over time (GGR) and the apparent
growth rate due to aging (AGR). Fortunately, the TE–age
line in 1870 can be compared to that in 1962-63 using the
data of table 3.6. The results are indeed enticing because of
the similarity in the two configurations. Wealth averages for

Chart 3.3. Cash Value per Farm in the United States from 1850 to 1960

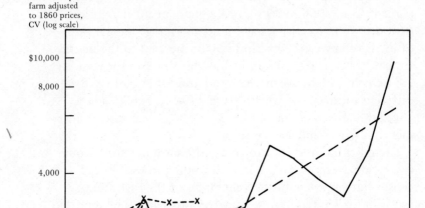

Cash value per
farm adjusted
to 1860 prices,
CV (log scale)

$10,000

8,000

4,000

North **X**

U.S.

2,000   South o

$$CV = \$2{,}110(1.013)^{t-1870}$$

1,000

1850   1870   1890   1910   1930   1950

Sources: Compendium of the 10th Census, 1880, pp. 650, 658; U.S. Census of Agriculture, 1964, vol. 2, chap. 1, p. 15. Cash value is deflated using the consumer price index; this is subject to criticism since factors causing changes in land values are complex.

Table 3.6. Average Wealth of Families and Unrelated Individuals in
1963 and Adult Males in 1870 in the United States
Classified by Age

	Average wealth		
Age	Adult males in 1870	Families and unrelated individuals in 1963	Ratio of average in 1963 to average in 1870
	(In current dollars)		
20-34	929	6,304	6.8
35-44	2,510	16,068	6.4
45-54	4,193	22,581	5.4
55-64	4,599	32,527	7.1
65 and up	5,128	30,838	6.0
All	2,399	20,982	8.7
	(In dollars adjusted to 1870 prices)		
20-34	929	2,600	2.8
35-44	2,510	6,600	2.6
45-54	4,193	9,200	2.2
55-64	4,599	13,000	2.9
65 and up	5,128	13,000	2.5
All	2,399	8,600	3.6

Sources: Spin sample of schedule 1 of the 1870 census; Board of
Governors of the Federal Reserve System as given in *Statistical Abstract of the United States, 1967,* p. 342. See also Dorothy S. Projector
and Gertrude S. Weiss, *Survey of Financial Characteristics of Consumers,* Federal Reserve Technical Papers. The price deflator is the
consumer price index taken in part from *Trends in the American
Economy in the Nineteenth Century,* ed. William N. Parker, vol. 24,
Studies in Income and Wealth, pp. 142, 143.

specific age groups today are between 5.4 and 7.1 times the
averages 93 years earlier, not considering price changes, and
between 2.2 and 2.9 times the averages of 93 years earlier if
adjustment is made by using the consumer price index. It is
remarkable that the 93-year ratios do not differ in essence.[31]

This is most significant in terms of the economic opportunities of the young and the old and the outlook of youth toward their elders. Those who maintain that events change more rapidly today than in earlier times cannot find evidence embedded in wealth differences among age groups. Accumulation of wealth in the private sector is allocated among people of age classes now as it was earlier.

The mean wealth in 1962-63 is larger than that in 1870, partly because the population is older. I calculate that the 1962-63 average would be only $14,900 if it were standardized by using age-specific populations of 1870 as weights.[32] If this standardized average and the 1870 $\overline{\text{TE}}$ of $2,399 are compared, an average annual rate of change of only 1.00 percent is obtained. The average annual rate of change of 1.38 percent for the 93 years would have been cut to 1.00 percent if the population had not aged. The growth rate from aging amounted to .3 or .4 percent a year. Our model for individual wealth in 1870 dollars now becomes $W = \$111(\text{adult age})(1.01)^{t-1870}$ if we consider the experience of the post-Civil War period. The annual growth factor of 1.0 percent (1.01 - 1.00) becomes 1.5 or 2.0 percent if we are dealing with the entire nineteenth century.

A Model of Apparent Growth Rates

Earlier in the chapter we studied two indexes of individual betterment. One was a wealth–age effect, measured as the apparent growth rate of wealth (AGR_W) of about 5 percent for each age year.[33] The other was general growth betterment per person of about 2 percent a year. Surely there must be a relationship between these two indexes and the fact that net population was growing 3 percent a year. If the wealth of those already in the labor force were 5 percent a year while there was a net infusion of men of 3 percent, we would expect per capita growth of $(1.05/1.03) - 1 = .02$. Let us now consider a more elaborate model in which deaths and estates of deceased are used.

Consider the arithmetic of a growth model in which growth rates per annum were .046 for gross population, .016 for deaths, .030 for net population, and .05 for wealth (AGR_N = .046 - .016 = .030, and AGR_W = .05). Let the population size (N) be 1,000, average wealth ($\overline{TE}$) be \$1,000, and the ratio of average wealth of deceased to average wealth of living be 1.5.

Start of the year:
$\quad$ N = 1,000, $\overline{TE}$ = \$1,000

End of the year:
$\quad$ N = 1,000, $\overline{TE}$ = \$1,050 $\quad\left\{\begin{array}{l}\text{die: } N_1 = \;\;16, \overline{TE}_1 = \$1{,}563 \\ \text{live: } N_2 = 984, \overline{TE}_2 = \$1{,}042\end{array}\right.$

Start of next year:
$\qquad\qquad\qquad$ estates of dead: $N_1\overline{TE}_1$
$\quad$ N = 1,030, $\overline{TE}$ = \$1,020 $\quad\left\{\begin{array}{l}\text{live: } N_2 = 984, \overline{TE}_2 = \$1{,}042 \\ \text{new: } N_3 = \;\;46, \overline{TE}_3 = \$0\end{array}\right.$

The living 984 do not have quite enough to support the 46 new young men with no wealth; the average is $(N_2\overline{TE}_2 + N_3\overline{TE}_3)/(N_2 + N_3)$ = 984 × \$1,042/1,030 = \$995. The estates of the dead raise the average by $N_1\overline{TE}_1 / (N_2 + N_3)$ = \$25. The new level is at \$995 + \$25 = \$1,020, a value 2.0 percent higher than the level one year earlier.

The figures used in the example are obtained from the study. Charts in chapter 1 show that age profiles in various census years implied gross population growth rates of about .041-.051. These implied net population growth, AGR_N, of .025-.035 when a death–inflation correction of .016-.017 was applied. The dimension of inheritance may be added by considering the wealth of those dying each year. This can be done by multiplying each age-specific wealth average by the corresponding age-specific death rate (or, more particularly, the wealth of each individual by his probability of dying). Suppose one applies Massachusetts or English death rates of the period[34] to the real or total estate figures for 1850-70. Aggregate estates of deceased amount to .020-.029 times

aggregate estates of the living. This aggregate inheritance
ratio seems to average about .025 ≈ (.016)(1.5), where
.016 is the average death rate of adults in a year and 1.5 is
the ratio of average wealth of deceased to the average wealth
of the living. The deceased had average adult age[35] and average real estate or total estate about 50 percent larger than
those for the adult living. Finally, the model has led to per
capita growth of approximately $AGR_W - AGR_N = .05 - .03$,
that is, the difference in the apparent growth rates of wealth
and population.[36]

Income Related to Wealth

Economists at midcentury were enamored of the dynamics
of saving with compound interest. Wealth might accumulate
very rapidly even though there were depreciation and
obsolescence. It was somewhat of a shock to Amasa Walker
in 1865, when he made his statistical estimate that wealth
was only 3.7 times as large as income. Part of the illusion
might have arisen because it was known that the wealth/in-
come ratio (W/Y) had been, and was, rising rapidly in Ohio
and to the west.[37] In the West, real estate values particularly
rose from very little to not much less than national values
in the decades preceding 1870.[38] My estimates of the ratio
at midcentury, using the adjusted estimates given earlier in
the chapter and Kuznets's estimates of income,[39] are
presented in the accompanying table.

	Mean TE, adjusted for slaves	Mean income per worker	W/Y
1850	$1,223	$399	3.1
1860	1,853	526	3.5
1870	2,399	737	3.3

At the time the ratio was apparently about 3.3, just about
the same as the 1962-63 ratio of $20,982/$6,378 = 3.3, as
estimated by the Federal Reserve group.[40]

An alternative procedure that may be used to estimate W/Y is based on the saving rate on income (s_Y) and the saving rate on wealth (s_W). Simon Kuznets has determined that the gross saving rate on income was about .20 in the period encompassing 1870.[41] It has been suggested that the saving rate on wealth is about .06, based on the wealth–age effect of .046-.052 per year and on general growth of .010-.020 per year. It must be true that $s_Y Y = s_W W$ if the amount saved from wealth is the same as that saved from income. The estimate of W/Y based on this equation is, then, roughly .20/.06, or 3.3.

It is interesting to make calculations of income based on W/Y and dollar savings as estimated from changes in wealth at different ages. The difference in mean wealth of those aged 48 and 47 in 1870 gives an estimate of the saving of men in their 48th year. Suppose the dollar saving in a year is $s_Y Y_{age} = \triangle \overline{TE}_{age} = \overline{TE}_{age} - \overline{TE}_{age-1}$, where $\triangle \overline{TE}$ is the incremental increase in mean wealth for an age group one year older than another. If s_Y and s_W do not change with age, then $\overline{Y}_{age}/\overline{Y} = \triangle \overline{TE}_{age}/(\triangle \overline{TE})$. The ratio $\overline{Y}_{age}/\overline{Y}$ is not known for 1870 but we can brazenly estimate it by using 1966 income data, as shown in table 3.7, column 2. We note that its wealth counterpart of $\triangle \overline{TE}_{age}/\triangle \overline{TE}$ (col. 5 of the table) is similar. (It is necessary to use the apparent growth rate of .047 in 1870 in the estimate of $\triangle \overline{TE} = .047\ \overline{TE}$ since we are dealing with change between age groups at a point in time.) We find the same patterns in the configurations for real estate in 1850 (col. 6), 1860, and 1870. Some correspondence has been shown between the slope of the wealth–age curve in midcentury and the income–age curve in 1966. Perhaps the income–age curve for midcentury had the same general shape; perhaps the propensity to save from income did not differ substantially among age groups.

The point of the above explanation is that income determines wealth. A more satisfactory explanation can be found

Table 3.7. Mean Incomes in 1966 and Wealth Increments in 1870 by Age

	Mean income			*Average wealth increments*		
	$\overline{Y}_{age}$	$\overline{Y}_{age}/\overline{Y}$	Y_{age}	$\triangle\overline{TE}_{age}$	$\triangle TE_{age}/\triangle TE$	
	1966	1966	1870	1870	1870	1850a
Age	(1)	(2)	(3)	(4)	(5)	(6)
18-24	$3,014	.5	$350	$ 36	.3	.3
25-34	6,935	1.1	700	97	.9	.7
35-44	8,257	1.3	810	118	1.1	1.2
45-54	8,098	1.3	960	169	1.5	1.3
55-64	6,825	1.1	940	41	.4	1.2
65-99	3,335	.5	790	53	.5	-.4
18-99	6,331	1.0	737	112	1.0	1.0

Sources: Column (1) is from Current Population Reports, *Consumer Income*, "Annual Mean Income, Lifetime Income, and Educational Attainment of Men in the United States for Selected Years, 1965-1966," series P-60, no. 56, Aug. 14, 1968, pp. 27, 28. The 1870 average income is from Kuznets, *Economic Growth and Structure*, p. 305. (3) = 737×(2), $\overline{\triangle TE}$ = AGR($\overline{TE}$) = .047($2,399) = $111 or the slope of the linear equation fitted to the mean wealth of age classes.

aEach ratio is $\overline{RE}_{age}/\triangle\overline{RE}$ using real estate values in 1850.

by turning the argument around in computing how much wealth one needs to provide income after retirement. If one accumulates 6 percent of his wealth annually, then after 40 years, at age 60, he has perhaps 2.5 times average wealth. If the interest rate is 5 percent and the total estate/income ratio is 3.3/1, his wealth in the form of an annuity at age 60 is sufficient for annual payments equivalent to average income for 10 years, or until he is 70. This explanation does add some plausibility to a rationale of a 6 percent saving rate.[42] Wealth is the goal because it is needed to provide retirement income.

Summary

Average wealth in the United States at midcentury was very substantial. It was 3-3.5 times income and by 1860 had

risen to about 30 percent of present average wealth.[43] Estimates of the growth in mean wealth for all adult males in
the United States are 3.1 percent a year from 1850 to 1860
and -.9 percent from 1860 to 1870. Mean total estate in
the North remained constant during the decade of the Civil
War while that in the South fell by a third. The average for
whites in the South dropped two-thirds because of the loss
of slave values and depressed real estate values.

The summary averages camouflage certain dynamic features of wealth accumulation of individuals. I have estimated
that the increase in wealth of an individual was about 6 percent a year. This was composed of two parts: (1) an apparent growth rate averaging 4.5-5.2 percent for each year
of adult life as determined from data in any given census
year, and (2) a general growth rate of 1.0-2.0 percent a year.
The average individual experienced strong growth in wealth
during his lifetime: wealth in his sixties was about 2.5 times
the mean wealth of all men.

There was a significant improvement in the relative position
of men in the urban sector during the decade of the Civil
War. Among whites over 40 in 1870, the mean wealth of
nonfarmers was greater than that of farmers. Foreign-born
whites had mean wealth little more than one-half that of
native-born whites at midcentury, but it was strictly an urban
disparity. The westward movement in northern states was
accompanied by an increase in mean wealth in the Northwest relative to mean wealth in the Northeast.

4. General Inequality: The Rich and Not-So-Rich

In the development of the United States, wealth has been distributed among men in a rather unequal fashion; it is the purpose of this chapter to describe how much wealth inequality actually existed at mid-nineteenth century. A beginning in this direction was made in chapter 2 when I used various classifications of men to portray how many poor there were, but nothing was said about distribution of wealth among those holding wealth. What proportion of total wealth was held by the top 1, 10, or 20 percent of wealthholders in a given year? Was there a plutocratic elite of 10, 100, or 1,000 men who held inordinate portions of total wealth? At midcentury, or for that matter, over the long time interval of the nineteenth and twentieth centuries, did the rich get richer even though the poor did not get poorer? An attempt to answer these questions constitutes the material of this chapter.

If one were to choose the decade in American history that would most likely produce change in economic inequality, he would surely have to select the decade of the Civil War. It is the purpose of this chapter to describe what took place in the area of wealth inequality. This will be accomplished by comparing real estate distribution in 1850 and 1860 and total estate distribution for the free in 1860 and whites in 1870. Wealth distribution of all in 1870 will be compared with wealth distribution today and with information on parts of total distribution at intervening points. Inequality in 1850 and 1860 will be compared with limited information on inequality in 1800.

Real Estate in 1850

There is no question that the rich *were* rich in the United States in 1850. Whether or not they were a real plutocracy

must be judged from the figures themselves. We find that
the top 1 percent of adult males held 30 percent of the real
estate of all adult males ($N_X = N_{RE} = .01; A_X = A_{RE} =$
.30) and that the top 2 percent held 40 percent of the total.
One tends to think of these figures as quantifications representing extreme concentration of wealth (real property).
This is because the 1 or 2 persons in a group of 100 would
seem to be such a select few. Yet the phenomenon simply
may stem from the fact that people usually can name fewer
than 500, or perhaps fewer than 100, adult males whom
they know. Some of the other key points in the 1850
distribution are presented in the accompanying table.

N_{RE}	A_{RE}
.05	.58
.10	.73
.20	.89
.41	1.00

Perhaps it is an exaggeration to say that the top 10 percent
or maybe 20 percent of men held almost all the real property
in America; nevertheless, there is an ample element of truth
in the statement. It is only because property value was so
large that the 11 percent of wealth held by middle groups
below the top 20th percentile is meaningful. It so happens
that the 20th percentile is located at the mean real estate of
$1,001; and a given percentile range of men below this level
does not have so much as a 1 percent share of wealth. A 1
percentile range of men has 1 or more percent of wealth
only if it is above the average. It is in this sense that only
one-fifth of men received at least a typical share.

   Relatively few people may be able to exert a strong economic influence in a small community; it may be human
nature to believe that a few people can then dominate regions
of the country in the economic sphere or to believe that the
country is dominated by a plutocracy. This reasoning is un-
justifiable if applied to America since one would have to
consider many more than a selected few if he wished to

demonstrate dominance. In 1850, 1 percent of the population of free adult males represents 50,000 men and such an
unwieldy number could hardly constitute a plutocracy.
Possibly 5,000 or, better still, 500 men might be considered
a ruling economic class, but these groups held, respectively,
only 10 percent and 3 percent of total wealth in the United
States. This was no England with 400 peers and peeresses
owning 17 percent of the land. In the English case fewer
than .5 percent of landowners—consisting of peers, great
landowners, and squires—owned half of all acreage.[1]

The 30 percent portion of wealth held by the top 1 percent may be contrasted with United States share figures of
32 percent for 1922 and 25 percent for 1953 found by
Robert Lampman. It is truly remarkable that the figures
for 1850 and 1922 are about the same. The Federal Reserve
Board reports shares of the top 1.28 percent of families in
1962-63, and our 1850 data, presented in the accompanying table, allow share determination of the same positions.

N_X	Federal Reserve A_X, 1962-63	Real estate A_X, 1850
.0036	.216	.192
.0128	.347	.336
.0248	.423	.442

The similarity of these results is quite astonishing. This is a
fruitful finding for purposes of comparison because it helps
us obtain a proper feeling for the relative opulence of the
economic elite at midcentury. If wer are not disturbed by
affluence at this level today, it is doubtful if we would have
been disturbed at that time, particularly because the communication and transportation systems would have made
the rich less noticeable. It must be understood that even 1
percent of a population represents a large number of people
and that the .1 percent or .01 percent might be the elite
groups about which people are concerned. There is evidence
that the proportionate shares held by these extremely select
groups was not much less in 1850 than today.[2]

I made a special sampling of the top .1 percent of real-holders in 1850 who had more than $60,000 in estate. This sample of 87 men had occupational titles such as

> farmer, planter, tobacconist, gentleman, landlord, hotel
> keeper, engineer, doctor, lawyer, clergyman, merchant,
> corn merchant, lumber merchant, grocer, dealer, miner,
> mason, manufacturer, ink manufacturer, charcoal manu-
> facturer, ship builder, machinist, watchmaker.

The representation among the realholder elite from southern states was the same as it was among the free population as a whole. There were greater numbers of foreign born among the select group than might be expected, including some of Irish, German, and French birth as well as those of English or Scottish birth. This was a contrast to the foreign-born representation below the top .1 percent. Some of the affluent, even in the North, lived very well if such a judgment can be made from the number of maids, waiters, servants, and laborers listed as parts of the households of the rich. Irish maids were particularly prevalent. Perhaps Tocqueville characterized the situation in America in the 1830s when he stated that a democracy will have some natural inequality: "The wealthy will not be so closely linked to each other as the members of the former aristocratic class of society; their inclinations will be different, and they will scarcely ever enjoy leisure as secure or complete."[3]

Real Estate in 1860 and 1870

The evidence presented in preceding chapters suggests great stability of patterns from year to year as each age cohort follows the patterns of previous cohorts. Surely our working hypothesis must be that the level of inequality of real estate holdings remained the same from decade to decade at mid-century. One might maintain that the Homestead Act of 1862 would lessen inequality since it allowed farmers to

acquire free farms of up to 160 acres by living on them for
five consecutive years. On the other hand the greater
emphasis on manufacturing and larger commercial ventures
might lead one to believe that real estate in factories, ware-
houses, and business establishments would lead to greater
concentration. However, these activities are not likely to
create radical changes in realholdings in the short run.

The figures of percentage shares are given in table 4.1 and
portrayed in chart 4.1. One observes first of all that there

Table 4.1. Relative Shares of Aggregate Real Estate Owned (A_{RE})
by Top Percentile Groups of Adult Men (N_{RE}) in 1850-70

N_{RE}	A_{RE}		
	1850	1860	1870 white
.0001	.03	.02	.02
.001	.10	.09	.06
.01	.30	.29	.24
.02	.40	.39	.34
.05	.58	.57	.52
.10	.73	.73	.70
.20	.89	.89	.88
.30	.97	.96	.96
.40	.99	.99	.99

Sources: Spin samples. See also table A4.

was *remarkable stability* in the portions held above given percentiles in 1850-60. This is our sole source of information
about inequality for that decade because we have no information on total estate shares for 1850. The figures are so close
that one can only conclude that inequality in 1840 and 1830
was similar but we shall need to do some further checking
for specific age groups. The second observation is that shares
of percentile groups in 1870 were basically the same as those
in 1860. There does seem to be a serious qualification for
those with N_{RE} between .001 and .05 since their shares

Chart 4.1. Inverse Pareto Curves of the Distribution of Real Estate among Free Adult Males in 1850
and 1860 and White Adult Males in 1870

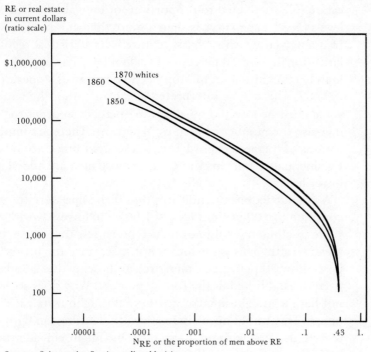

RE or real estate
in current dollars
(ratio scale)

Sources: Spin samples. See Appendix table A4.

dropped. However, those in the 5th to 20th percentiles picked up the slack, so the overall picture remained the same.

Realholder Pareto Curves

The Pareto curves of chart 4.1 represent a standard technique for showing wealth distributions. Various levels of estate (X) are related to proportions of men above these levels (N_X). Each curve is then a more than cumulative frequency curve whose basic feature is its statistical regularity for the top 10 percent of realholders. The approximately straight line in the top decile range gives slopes of .60–.67. This can be interpreted as meaning that the wealth value must be lowered by about .67 percent in order to increase the number of men by 1 percent. There are implications of hierarchical order with a straight line since relative inequality remains the same as more men are added at lower levels.[4]

A graphic extension indicates that if the line were to continue to 100 percent (N_X = 1.00), the lowest wealth value of all men would not be too much less than the actual mean wealth. This is obviously not true, since the lower 90 percent or 80 percent of men drop well below the standard pattern established in the top 10 percent. Why does society not have a straight-line Pareto curve throughout its entire range? This would necessitate a wealth distribution with a reverse J shape with no lower tail. One might consider the basic shape of almost all frequency distributions of men classified by various characteristics such as mental ability, strength, desire, or luck. There always seems to be a lower tail. Wealth presents a further complication because it comes from saving, which can occur only after certain basic consumption standards have been met.

Total Estate in 1860 and 1870

Total estate is the most comprehensive measure that can be used in ascertaining inequality change from 1860 to 1870 even though slave values are included in the personal estate of southerners in 1860. (The wealth declarations on schedule 1 of the census did not indicate the number or value of slaves owned.[5]) Changes in inequality in the North are quite valid and deserve particular attention. Inequality changes affecting free in 1860 and whites in 1870 in the South and in the United States are valid in demonstrating the realignment of the economic values of the white man.

Table 4.2. Top Percentile Groups of Adult Males ($100N_{TE}$) and Their Percentage of Aggregate Total Estate ($100A_{TE}$) in 1860 and 1870

N_{TE}	A_{TE}, North			A_{TE}, South			A_{TE}, U.S.		
	1860	1870 white	1870 all	1860	1870 white	1870 all	1860	1870 white	1870 all
.001	.08	.06	.06	.07	.08	.10	.08	.06	.07
.010	.27	.24	.24	.27	.29	.33	.29	.25	.27
.020	.37	.34	.34	.39	.39	.44	.40	.35	.37
.050	.53	.51	.51	.59	.57	.62	.57	.52	.54
.100	.68	.67	.67	.75	.70	.77	.73	.68	.70
.200	.84	.84	.84	.89	.85	.91	.86	.85	.87
.300	.92	.93	.93	.95	.92	.96	.94	.93	.95
.400	.97	.97	.97	.98	.96	.99	.97	.97	.98
.500	.99	.99	.99	.99	.99	.99	.99	.99	.99

Sources: Spin samples.

Table 4.2 lists the shares held by individuals above various percentiles in the North in 1860 or 1870. There is evidence that the portion held by the top 5 percent diminished a little but this 5 percent was composed of those from the 5th to 20th percentiles (from the top). My general conclusion is that the *distribution of wealth in the North remained essentially the same during the Civil War decade.* One must be careful to note that this analysis treats a changing population that grew by 30 percent for all adult males and by 34 percent for foreign-born males in the 10 years, and one whose native-born population was depleted substantially among younger age groups.

Let us focus next on the change in inequality within the South. Whites had a little less inequality in 1870 than in 1860 except for the top 2-5 percent of men. This is extraordinary when one considers that the real value of mean wealth dropped by two-thirds. Inequality then was a very robust phenomenon. It is doubtful that there will ever be such a revolutionary change again within our society—and yet it left the relative hierarchy of whites as it was before. Some groups such as planters probably suffered while certain urban groups gained within the context of greatly deflated wealth values. The southern picture for *all* free men is our first accounting with former slaves now counted as freemen. They were generally at the bottom of the southern wealth distribution so we should expect large inequality in the South, and, in fact, the top 1-2 percent of men had 33-43 percent of all wealth. This share is large relative to the 24-34 percent held by the corresponding group in the North.

Finally, we turn to the United States as a whole. The figures of table 4.2 for the free of 1860 and whites of 1870 indicate a significant decrease in inequality for the top decile class, more so than for the case of the North. The second decile group is the recipient of increased shares, and inequality remained essentially the same for the lower 80 percent of white males. Negroes, in accounting for about 11 percent of all free men in 1870, did have a measurable impact on inequality. Their presence meant that the top 20 percent had shares 2 points higher than otherwise; an example is that the top 1 percent had A_X of .27 instead of .25. The addition of nonwhites does not significantly alter

the overall statistical picture of inequality. Of more impact on the picture in the United States is the fact that
southern planters were a dominant influence among the
economic elite in 1860 but not in 1870. This can be illustrated with the figures on residence in the accompanying
table.[6]

The rich of the U.S. (N_{TE} range)	Percentage of men from the South	
	1860 free	1870 all
.01 and up	59	18
.02 to .011	55	16
.05 to .021	42	19
.10 to .051	34	16
.20 to .101	25	21
1.00 and up	28	33

The statistics portray in a very dramatic way how the economic elite of the country was dominated by southerners
in the antebellum period. Three of every five men were
from the South in 1860 compared to one of every five after
the war. There were 70,000 Americans in 1860 with wealth
of $40,000 or more, and 40,000 of that number lived in the
South. There were 7,000 Americans (N_X = .001) with wealth
of $111,000 or more, 4,500 of whom lived in the South.
The southern plutocracy was destroyed by the Civil War, at
least in terms of the ownership of the country's private
wealth.

Wealthholder Lorenz Curves and Gini Coefficients

A standard procedure for displaying inequality has been
developed that highlights the poor and their share of wealth.
These individuals and their wealth may be plotted as a
Lorenz curve using $1 - N_X$ and $1 - A_X$ as the measures, as
shown in chart 4.2. An example of a point on the curve for
1860 is the plot where the lower 80 percent of free men
owned 14 percent of total wealth. The chart shows that there

Chart 4.2. Lorenz Curves of the Distribution of Wealth in the United States among Free Males 20 and Older in 1860 and 1870 and among Families in 1962-63

Proportion of
total estate, 1- A_{TE}

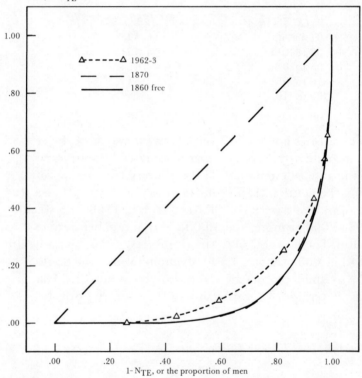

1- N_{TE}, or the proportion of men

Sources: Spin samples and Dorothy S. Projector and Gertrude S. Weiss, *Survey of Financial Characteristics of Consumers,* pp. 110, 151.

was little practical difference between the distribution of
wealth in 1860 and in 1870. There is an almost impercepti-
ble crossing of the two curves, with less inequality in the
upper tail of the 1870 distribution.

The Lorenz curve for a year would appear as the diagonal
line of the chart if perfect equality existed. The extent of
inequality may be measured by the area between the
diagonal line and the actual Lorenz curve for a year. This
area of inequality could be as large as the triangular area.
Let us define the Gini coefficient of inequality, G, as the
area of inequality divided by the triangular area under the
diagonal representing perfect inequality. G for all persons
in 1870 was .833, a ratio substantially far along in the
spectrum from G = 0 (perfect equality) to G = 1 (perfect
inequality). The fact that there were so many without
wealth boosted the inequality area appreciably; G for those
with wealth above $100 was only .706.

The Gini coefficient gives us an overall measure of relative inequality or relative dispersion of wealth at a point in
time that may be compared easily to that at any other point
indicated by the important values listed in table 4.3. Note

Table 4.3. Inequality Coefficients (G) of the Distribution of Total
Estate among Adult Males in 1860-70

	1860 free	1870 whites	1870 all
United States	.832	.814	.833
North	.813	.810	.816
South	.845	.818	.866

Sources: Spin samples.

that *inequality in the United States for all men in 1870 was
the same as it was for free men in 1860.* (Certainly the very
slight intersection of the two Lorenz curves is not a serious
qualification to this most significant finding.) The easiest
explanation is that inequality in the decade remained constant in the North but decreased among whites in the South

to the level in the North, primarily because of the destruction of slave values among the rich. The addition of former slaves brought southern inequality back above its former level. The coefficient for the United States was closer to that of the North in 1870 than in 1860 because there was relatively so much more wealth in the North in 1870.

It should be reported that relative inequality of real estate remained constant at midcentury. The Gini coefficient was .86 in 1850, .85 in 1860, .84 for whites in 1870, and .86 for all in 1870. A tremendous expansion in the population and a devastating war somehow left the real estate pie cut into the same portions. The nonslave population of 5 million adult males in 1850 became, with the addition of former slaves, one of 10 million in 1870. The figures for 1850 and 1860 lead one to believe that G for total estate remained constant in the same decade. This conclusion is strengthened by the fact that the rich in 1860 did not hold disproportiona amounts of real estate. Perhaps G for real estate and total estate remained constant for many years before and after midcentury.

Characteristics of the Rich and Poor

Occupations of the very rich in 1860 were similar to those fo 1850 with perhaps a few more titles such as real estate agent, builder, and contractor. Titles for the rich in 1870 do include the term *manufacturer* more often than did those for 1860. Consider the men in the United States in 1870 with $10,000 or more wealth, the group constituting the top 5 percent. These men were relatively old with an average age of 49 and had relatively fewer foreign born among them. The percentag of farmers among them was only slightly lower than among the population as a whole, and their real estate was two-thirds of their wealth—the same fraction that existed for the population as a whole. It seems that the rich as a whole were no more likely to represent or favor urban over rural interests or to represent disproportionately the interests of personal estate holders.[7]

America had pockets of extremely affluent people at mid-century. Let us examine two of them in 1860: Adams (Natchez) County, Mississippi, and Newport County, Rhode Island. Adams County contained an adult male population of 1,731 whites and 53 free colored. Of these, 50 were in America's select 7,000 men, with total estates of $111,000 or more ($N_{\$111,000} = .001$). Several of them living in the city of Natchez had more than 20 slaves each, an index of regal living.[8]

The North also had congregations of rich people in 1860. Newport County in June of 1860 had an adult male population of 5,702. Ten of these men made the select list of 7,000 and 5 more were very close. Of these 15, 8 had the title of gentleman. The number of servants in these families might give us the index of their style of living. The average number of servants was 4.5. While one lawyer with wealth of $525,000 had 10 servants, two millionaires had but 4 and 5 servants. Naturally there were areas of cities with concentrations of rich men. For example, the Eighteenth Ward of the Fourth District of New York City listed 2,300 adult men; 11 of them were in our royal 7,000, 5 with titles of gentleman and 4 with titles of merchant.[9]

Age, Occupation, and Nativity

The relationship between mean wealth and age presented in the preceding chapter presumably is dominated by the relatively few rich above the arithmetic mean at each age level. The wealth–age pattern should be tested for lower groups by excluding the rich from the computations. The results of eliminating successive layers of rich from the calculation of the mean are shown in chart 4.3. The straight-line patterns persist even after we remove the rich in the top 20 percent of the distribution ($P_0 - P_{100}$). The slopes of the lines

Chart 4.3. Mean Total Estate in 1870 for Adult Males within Given Wealth Percentiles (P_0-P_{100})

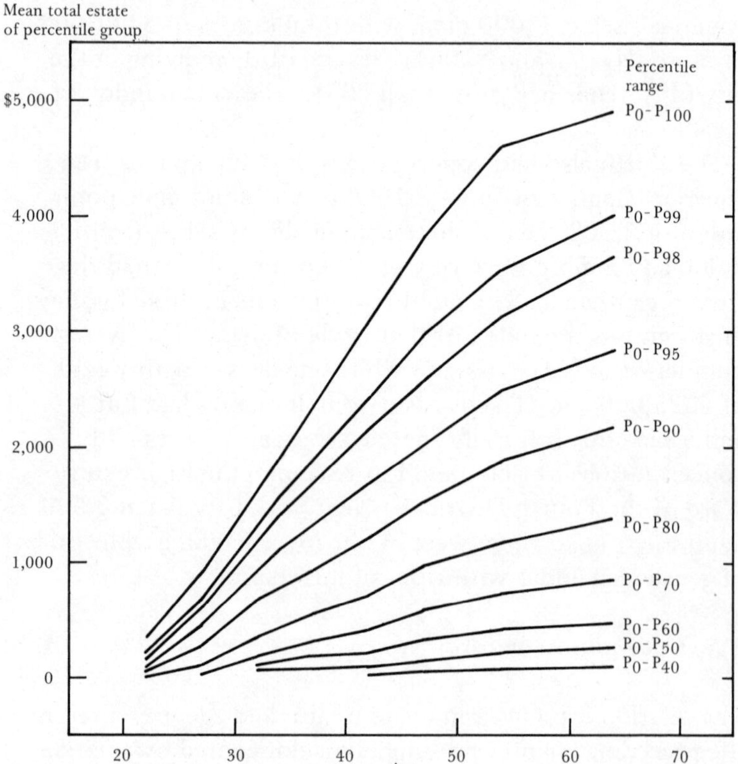

Sources: Spin samples.

continue to be about 4.5-5.0 percent of the average wealth of the subset; the apparent growth rates for wealth hold for lower groups but average wealth is very small.

The Gini coefficient of inequality of .833 for 1870 has been described as a general measure of the degree of concentration of wealth among men. Let us see what the coefficient is for various subsets obtained from classifying men by our three main variables. Table 4.4 indicates that the coefficient is high for the young in age group 20-29 and then is relatively constant from age 30 to 99. Not shown is

Table 4.4. Inequality Coefficients (G) of the Distribution of Total Estate among All Adult Males in the United States in 1870 by Age, Nativity, and Occupation

	Age			
	20 and up	20-29	30-39	40-99
All persons	.833	.90	.78	.78
Native born	.831	.89	.77	.77
Foreign born	.840	.89	.80	.81
Farmers	.765	.87	.72	.69
Native born	.777	.88	.73	.70
Foreign born	.683	.80	.62	.65
Nonfarmers	.886	.92	.82	.85
Native born	.880	.91	.81	.84
Foreign born	.888	.91	.84	.87

Source: Spin sample of 9,823.

the fact that it often decreases from age 30-39 to age 40-69 and then rises a little for those above 70. There is then a tendency for the pattern to be slightly curvilinear, particularly in the case of real estate. An example is the inequality of real estate in 1850, which is shown by the accompanying table.

Age	G
20-29	.92
30-39	.82
40-49	.81
50-59	.77
60-69	.77
70-99	.81

Table 4.4 reflects the fundamental fact that inequality was substantially less for farmers (G = .76) than for non-farmers (G = .89). There is no question that the elite of urban society had greater shares than did the elite of rural society. Consider the figures in the accompanying table for 1870.

Proportion of men, N_{TE}	Share of wealth, A_{TE}	
	Farmers	*Nonfarmers*
.001	.04	.08
.010	.17	.35
.020	.26	.48
.050	.42	.67
.100	.59	.81
.200	.79	.93
.400	.95	.99

The elite top 1 percent of urban residents owned 35 percent of urban wealth in 1870. The top 2 percent owned almost half of urban wealth! Contrast this to the rural sector, where shares for top percentile ranges were only half as large. One should note, however, that the distinction really involves the rich and near-rich but not those in the bottom half of the distribution. In urban areas those in the second and third decile ranges had little wealth relative to those in the first decile range of the distribution. We observe that a great part of wealth is accounted for in the first four decile ranges of both the urban and rural frequency curves. To say that mean wealth was the same in rural and urban areas of the country in 1870 is to camouflage strong differences. There were more farmers with wealth at moderate levels and fewer farmers with wealth at very high levels compared to the distributions for nonfarmers. The break-even value was $13,000 since each group had 3.5 percent of its members above this level. One might state that generally the probability was only 3.5 percent that an individual would have more wealth if he chose to live in an urban society; if he succeeded, he was rewarded handsomely.[10]

The coefficients of table 4.4 for all persons demonstrate the interesting fact that relative inequality was the same for both native- and foreign-born populations. The Lorenz curves for the two groups were quite similar but the curve for native-born whites had a little less inequality than that for foreign-born whites. An intriguing insight stems from the Gini coefficients of .833 for all men and .831 for native born. Inequality in the United States was almost the same whether or not one considered the foreign-born population! This was also true for urban areas of the country, where values of G were .886 for all and .880 for native born. The elimination of an important subset can introduce a strong paradox. Obviously, there is extreme inequality in the difference between the mean wealth of native and foreign born; one would quickly cite the foreign born as a major element contributing to inequality in urban areas. Yet statistical inequality of wealth among native born is almost as great as that for the group as a whole.[11] This paradox about some of the literature on inequality today is disturbing because differences in *average* wealth of majority and minority groups are significant even though there is wide dispersion within each group.[12]

Regression Equations and Projections

It is desirable to construct an equation that will relate the Gini coefficient to our important variables. I computed G for each of about 400 subsets of a cross-classification table having approximately 50 age classes, 2 nativity, 2 occupation, and 2 residence classes; these G values were then correlated by weighting each cell by the number of cases in that cell. This procedure yields the following equations for total estate, age, and three dichotomous variables for all adult males in the United States in 1870:

$$G = .889 - .0051 \text{ age} + .1100 \text{ nA} - .0151 \text{ FB} + .0535 \text{ So.}$$

The coefficients tell us that inequality decreases with age, increases with urbanity (nA = 1 for nonfarmers), actually decreases if one is foreign born (FB = 1), and is higher if one lives in the South (So = 1). Two major long-run determinants of interest are age and urbanity. If the difference in average age between young and old is 25 years, the magnitude of age inequality cancels that of urban inequality in the above equation. Suppose the proportion of urban men increases .40 in a century from .52 to .92; the equation would tell us that this would increase inequality by .40 × .1100, or .044. Assume at the same time that the male average age increases 6.6 years; the equation says this would decrease inequality by 6.6 × .0051, or .034. Thus, the aging of the population could have produced a quantitative effect in the last century (1870-1960) that counteracted the effect of urbanity. There is little in the equation to suggest change during the century. The specter of increased inequality in the country has been based on the urban movement. The countervailing effect of an aging population has been neglected. There is no reason to believe that aging is any more alien to settlement than is the urban movement.[13]

The two multiple regression equations for inequality of total estate among whites in 1870 and free in 1860 display an astonishing constancy for a decade suffering the most violent disruption in our history.

1870 whites: $G_{TE} = .873 - .0052$ age $+ .126$ nA $- .007$ FB $+ .014$ So

1860 free: $G_{TE} = .871 - .0044$ age $+ .116$ nA $- .017$ FB $+ .031$ So

These two equations might be regarded as the most important in this book for persons considering the general organization of men or their power over economic resources. Some changes are not overpowering in overall quantitative terms. The effect of urbanity on G is increased slightly in the decade, but this effect is negated by a drop in the influence of the foreign born on inequality. The equation for all in 1870 is startlingly

close to that for free in 1860 except for the expected increase in inequality in the South brought about by treating
nonwhites as humans for the first time.

Inequality since 1800

Writers at the end of the nineteenth century concluded that
the rich were getting richer even if the poor were not so
poor.[14] They did so by observing the growth of millionaires
in the upper one-tenth of 1 percent of the population who
had made their money in coal, iron, and oil, using the
mechanisms of securities and trusts. G. P. Watkins wrote in
a 1907 publication of the American Economic Association:

> If modern tendencies are such as favor the growth of
> large fortunes, we should expect the United States to
> be more fertile in the production of these than any
> other country. This is fundamentally what accounts for
> the fact that the United States, once the land of eco-
> nomic equality, is now the land of millionaires.[15]

In 1927 the Beards described the Gilded Age after the
Civil War as one of "spreading plutocracy" and the "triumph
of lucre."[16] Matthew Josephson in his 1934 book *The
Robber Barons* perhaps has done more in shaping the present
belief that the rich obtained an increasing share in the last
half of the nineteenth century. He rests his case primarily
on a list of 12 men but interestingly two of them, James
Fisk and Cornelius Vanderbilt, died in 1872 and 1877,
respectively, and the list does not include John Jacob Astor,
who died in 1848.[17]

It is true that 10 or 20 men gained spectacular wealth by
1900 or, more accurately, by 1920 or later. Nevertheless,
an overemphasis on this fact has distorted our view of the
fundamental inequality framework of wealth ownership in
America. These few men did have economic power that
strongly transcended ownership, but this situation prevailed

also in 1870 and, for that matter, in 1970. It is my hypothesis that general inequality in the ownership of wealth remained relatively constant until 1900 and possibly 1920. It has probably decreased since that time but perhaps only since 1940. The evidence will be based on shares of wealth of upper wealth groups after 1922, wealth distributions in 1870 and 1962-63, mortgage distributions from 1880 to 1889, a farm and home census of 1890, and Indiana inequality from 1870 to 1900.

Millionaires

The Beards were willing to highlight, even with some doubt, the statement that the number of millionaires in the United States was perhaps 3 in 1861 and at least 3,800 in 1897.[18] We are now in a much better position to authenticate the actual trend in the growth of millionaires over time. The spin samples of adult males in census manuscripts yield an estimated 41 millionaires in 1860 and 545 millionaires in 1870. Although it is true that these figures are subject to wide sampling error, each is part of a fairly smooth Pareto curve. (I will show later that Pareto curves for the very rich are similar in 1870 and 1962.) The next firm estimate of the number of millionaires is 5,904 for 1922, as determined by Robert Lampman.[19] The number has grown since that time to 60,000-67,000 in 1962, as estimated by the Bureau of Internal Revenue.[20]

Is the number in 1870 really out of line with the number in 1922? Consider three effects of change in the 55-year period for which we need adjustment: (1) Prices were 1.35 times as large in 1922. (2) Per capita wealth was between 1.7 and 2.3 times as large if the rate of real growth were 1.0-1.5 percent a year. The rich, as well as the poor, should share in economic growth. (3) The population was 3.5 times as large in 1922. The first two factors lead to the calculation that a wealth level of $330,000-$430,000 in

1870 was the equivalent of $1 million in 1922. There were 1,800-2,600 men with wealth above this limit in 1870. Because population was greater, we would expect between 6,400 and 9,400 millionaires in 1922 on the basis of the data for 1870! These figures are as high as Lampman's estimate of 5,904 for 1922.

Similar calculations for the period 1870-1962 produce estimates of 54,000-74,000 for the number of millionaires in 1962, a range that encompasses the reported number in that year. This procedure has also been employed with incomes from the 1866-71, 1914, and 1965 income tax returns for incomes above $100,000; again, it has been found that the number for the century are consistent following the three adjustments.[21]

There must have been a millionaire mirage because people did not realize that economic growth and population growth affected the number of rich. This is not to deny the fact that there were a few exceedingly rich men. But even if Andrew Carnegie garnered $500 million before giving it away, he would have accounted for only .5 percent of total wealth. The extension of the 1870 Pareto curve to the top man would not be out of line with this figure. For income tax purposes in New York City in 1864, the top two incomes reported were $1.843 million by A. T. Stewart and $838,000 by William B. Astor. If Stewart's income were capitalized at 5 percent, it would yield wealth of $36 million. Inflation, productivity, and population increases could easily make this the counterpart of $100 million fifty years later.

We note finally in table 4.5 that there is a striking correspondence between the distribution of wealth among the very rich in 1870 and 1962. The slope of the inverse Pareto line for these points was .667 in both years. Thus the Pareto curves are very similar for rich people. Estate tax distributions for net estates of deceased above $100,000 are available from 1916 to 1941 for the United States. I have

Table 4.5. Cumulative Percentage Shares of Net Worth above
$60,000 in 1962 (100N$_{NW}$) and of Total Estate above
$6,000 in 1870 (100N$_{TE}$) of Rich Males in the United
States

1962		1870		
Net worth, *NW*	*100N$_{NW}$*	*Total estate,* *TE*	*100N$_{TE}$*	*N$_{NW}$/N$_{TE}$*
$10,000,000	.0021	$1,000,000	.0056	.38
5,000,000	.0044	500,000	.014	.32
2,000,000	.019	200,000	.049	.38
1,000,000	.057	100,000	.15	.37
500,000	.17	50,000	.53	.32
200,000	.69	20,000	2.1	.33
100,000	1.9	10,000	5.4	.34
60,000	3.3	6,000	10.	.33

Sources: Spin sample of 9,823 and a partial list of 165 rich individuals
above $100,000; the 1962 data are from U.S. Treasury Department,
Internal Revenue Service *Personal Wealth Estimated from Estate Tax
Returns,* supplemental report of May 1967, pp. 20, 35; a population
of 55.0 million males 20 and older was used as a base.

combined various years to obtain the slopes[22] presented in
the accompanying table.

	Inverse Pareto *slope*	*Number of net estate* *classes considered*
1916-21	.70	15
1922-23	.70	15
1925-26	.73	13
1928-31	.78	18
1932-34	.65	18
1936	.70	14
1938	.69	18
1941	.70	24

The evidence here is that inequality increased in the 1920s
but that there was no general shift in the level from World
War I to World War II. Gross estate distributions of deceased
above $60,000 have been published since 1938. Their slopes

indicate decreased inequality until the 1950s; this confirms the findings of Robert Lampman concerning the shares of the top group of families.[23]

Lorenz Curves in 1870 and 1962-63

Chart 4.2 shows Lorenz curves for wealth of families and unrelated individuals in 1962-63 along with that for adult males in 1870. It can be seen that between the 40th and 90th percentiles there is less inequality today than a century earlier but that the curves are otherwise the same. The fact that the Gini coefficient was .76 in 1962-63 and .83 in 1870 means that inequality has dropped. If we subsume within the families those adult males with no wealth who were in families with wealth, the .83 could possibly drop to .80 or .81.[24] Perhaps wealth in 1963 was 5 percent less concentrated than in 1870. Furthermore, one could build a case for stating that a sizable part of this remaining difference could be explained by the fact that there were not so many youths in the population. The fact that the population was 6.6 years older (see pp. 109–10) could make G smaller by .034 points.

Mortgages, 1880-89

The Bureau of the Census made an elaborate study of mortgage values for each year from 1880 to 1889. The data included all mortgages except those made by quasipublic corporations such as railroad, telegraph, and public water companies. A large proportion of the mortgages were obtained for the purpose of acquiring land. The mortgage transactions were a peculiarly sensitive index of the transfer of properties since the average length of a mortgage was only about 4 years. Each year a very detailed frequency distribution was presented from which the Gini coefficient was computed. I present an abridged form for 1889 in the accompanying table.

Lower class limit	Number of mortgages
$ 0	804,461
1,000	400,121
10,000	19,939
100,000	1,802
	1,226,323

The Gini coefficients in table 4.6 indicate that there was strong stability in financial mortgage distribution connected with real estate and business transactions in the United States in the second decade after 1870.

Table 4.6. Mean and Inequality Coefficients of Real Estate Mortgage Values in the United States, 1880-89

	Mean	Gini G		Mean	Gini G
1880	$1,105	.642	1885	$1,164	.638
1881	1,184	.650	1886	1,241	.652
1882	1,262	.656	1887	1,347	.658
1883	1,243	.650	1888	1,353	.663
1884	1,227	.652	1889	1,429	.666

Sources: U.S. Census Bureau, 11th Census, 1890, *Mortgages,* vol. 12 (Washington, D.C., 1895), pp. 750-51. See also Lee Soltow, *Patterns of Wealthholding in Wisconsin,* pp. 116-17.

Farm and Home Census of 1890

In the 1890 census each family occupying a farm or home was asked whether or not the family was an owner or tenant and the value and debt of the farm or home if it was encumbered. We can make an approximation of an overall farm and home distribution by using the relative dispersion and equity value of the encumbered owners, and the number of unencumbered, encumbered, tenants, and males 20 and older. From this estimate I obtained Gini coefficients of .79 for farmers, .89 for nonfarmers, and .85 for all persons.[25] (I made these computations long before results were available from the spin samples.) The spin-sample coefficients for real estate of all males in 1870 were .79 for farmers, .91 for nonfarmers, and .86 for all men. We can accept these statistics as important evidence that inequality in the United States in 1890 was about the same as it was in 1870.

Indiana Appraisals, 1870-1900

The Indiana Department of Statistics compiled distributions of wealth for 1870-1900 based on the quadrennial appraisement of real estate and the annual valuation of personal property and improvements of all individuals in all the counties. Real estate valuation was two-thirds of the total valuation in each year. Frequency tables of 24 wealth classes were published for each of the 92 counties.[26] I have collated these tables for the state to obtain the figures in the accompanying table.

	Gini coefficient, G	Number of values	Mean wealth	
			Current dollars	1860 dollars
1870	.684	489,285	1,249	1,249
1880	.697	617,116	1,097	1,410
1890	.707	737,480	1,067	1,460
1900	.708	909,654	1,184	1,760

These four separate estimates of inequality show constancy of wealth inequality in the last third of the nineteenth century.

Southern States before 1860

A study of taxable holdings of males 21 and older in Kentucky in 1800 was reported briefly in chapter 2. The definition of wealth was quite comprehensive because the individual reported to the county authority the land, horses, slaves, stores, taverns, and carriages owned, no matter where they were located in the state. Each of these categories was weighted by tax rates representing relative market values to obtain the tax assessment for the individual. The Gini coefficient of inequality for the distribution of these values

among free males was .81. The G values for total estate in
Kentucky were .83 for free men in 1860 and .83 for white
men in 1870. Lorenz curves cross one another slightly with
greater shares held by the top few percent in 1800. The
conclusion is that wealth inequality in Kentucky was the
same in 1800, 1860, and 1870.

I computed inequality coefficients for the distributions
of slaves in the South from 1790 to 1860. The Gini coefficient for slaves among slaveholders in four states was
.602 in 1790, .599 in 1830, .595 in 1850, and .600 in
1860. Some of the coefficients will be described further in
the next chapter. The results reveal constancy of inequality
in the southern states for 1790-1860.[27] Statistical evidence
for the North must come mostly from probated estates and
assessed valuation. The slope of the inverse Pareto curves
for Massachusetts probated estates with inventories were
similar in 1829-31 and 1859-61.[28] Perhaps the best statement of recognition of the problem is that given in 1826 by
Langston Byllesby, a Philadelphia printer and journalist:
"The tendency of the existing systems to an oppressive
Inequality of Wealth, together with its unstable character
and disorders arising therefrom, have frequently undergone
the discussion of able men."[29]

The available evidence indicates that inequality of wealth
remained the same from 1800 to 1940 and then decreased
a little, particularly among middle-wealth groups. There was
an emergence of a plutocratic elite with extraordinary wealth
at the turn of the century but this phenomenon involved,
at most, a score of people. It did not fundamentally alter
the share of wealth held by the top 1 percent of persons.
The main consideration is that there already was strong inequality in 1860 and 1870.

Lognormal Distribution

The distribution of wealth has been characterized up to this
point in terms of a Lorenz curve and an inverse Pareto curve.

The latter shape has the appearance of a straight line for the top .1 percent of the cases and roughly a straight line for the top 10 percent. An alternative statistical form can be used to describe fairly accurately the distribution of total estate among those having positive values.[30] If one takes the logarithm of each person's total estate in 1870, he finds that the resulting frequency distribution is almost exactly normal.[31] The accompanying table reports the proportion of cases from the mean in standard deviation units.

r, or number of standard deviations from mean	N_r, or the proportion of cases above r	
	Actual	Normal curve
+3	.0015	.0014
+2	.023	.023
+1	.163	.159
0	.497	.500
−1	.834	.841
−2	.993	.997
−3	.999	.999

This marvelous fit gives us verification that percentage differentials are appropriate in characterizing distribution of wealth. An example for 1870 is that there were approximately as many cases between $500 and $1,000 as there were between $1,000 and $2,000 and approximately as many between $100 and $1,000 as between $1,000 and $10,000. This does not give us any causal explanation of why one individual is one standard deviation above the mean while another is the same distance below the mean. If an individual has superior ability or physique or luck in accumulating capital, he may very well be above the mean instead of below it. The danger of the concept of the lognormal distribution is that it implies that the distribution is a matter of chance. Of all individuals, half might succeed at a given venture and half fail. After the second trial, one-fourth may have succeeded twice, one-half once, and one-fourth may not have succeeded at all. We have an incipient binomial or normal distribution that may be made lognormal if rewards are in percentages.[32] As a consequence, the outcome may be attributed to luck or chance.

Distribution of Saving

It would be desirable to describe the saving of people in a given year as a beginning step in understanding their saving, consumption, and income. The task undertaken here is to estimate the annual distribution of saving by men on the basis of total estate figures. Suppose one made the assumption, based on the linear relationship demonstrated earlier in the chapter, that total estate divided by the number of adult years gives saving $[S = TE/(age - 18)]$.[33] If an individual of age 38 in 1870 had a TE of $1,000, his saving would be estimated as $50 for the year. This transformation was made by computer for each man in 1870 with the results below:

	Mean	Gini G
Wealth	$2,399	.833
Saving	111	.823

Note that inequality of saving is almost the *same* as inequality of wealth. The ratio of means, $\overline{S}/\overline{TE}$, is .046, the same as our apparent growth rate for total estate given in the preceding chapter. Since saving has been estimated from a cross section in one year, it might be appropriate to add a per capita growth element of .01 or .02 percent in boosting saving from $111 to roughly $140.

An alternative procedure for measuring saving would be to compute the percentage differential between two age groups $[(\overline{TE}_{age}/\overline{TE}_{age-1}) - 1]$ and apply this to each man's wealth. This transformation was run and it was again found that the distribution of relative saving was the same as that for wealth. These estimates may very well be superior to those found from income and consumption studies for one year. My estimate gives an average of an individual's annual savings for a series of years.

Distribution of Income

The commissioner of Internal Revenue reported the number of people in five or six income classes in each of the years 1866-71 as derived from income tax returns. All these upper-tail data had inverse Pareto slopes of about .67, the same slope as found for wealth distribution among the rich.[34] Information is not available for middle- or lower-income classes but it is certainly expected that the ratios of wealth to income and of saving to income decrease to zero among the poor. It is not unreasonable to believe that the general form of the entire income curve might be derived from the information available from savings figures for a year such as 1870. I shall describe a succinct outline of a possible procedure for doing this.

We can construct an income distribution with desirable characteristics from the saving distribution if a reasonable consumption function can be established. A study of the 1962-63 figures for income and saving[35] leads to the idea that there is a threshold T at about one-third of mean income, below which there is no saving and that those with income Y above the threshold have consumption C from optional income of $C = (Y - T)^{.95}$. A computer run was made for those with positive saving by use of the transformation $Y = S + C = S + (Y - .33\overline{Y})^{.95}$, where Y may be determined solely from the saving estimate. Those without saving were distributed evenly from an income of 0 to T.[36] The resulting income distribution has $\overline{S}/\overline{Y}$ of about .20, a ratio similar to Kuznets's gross domestic capital formation rate.[37] Now, if $\overline{S}$ is $140, then $\overline{Y}$ is $700 and $T = .33\overline{Y} =$ $270. These values are realistic because Kuznets has estimated income per worker as $737 in 1870[38] and $270 was about the wage rate of a farm hand in 1870.[39]

The income distribution above is only one possibility but it does have an upper-tail Pareto slope similar to that revealed by the 1866-71 income tax figures, the rectangular distribution below the threshold is consistent with observed income distribution in the lower tail today, and there is no real discontinuity in frequency density just above or below T. The Gini coefficient of inequality for income is about .60. Thus, inequality for wealth and saving of about .83 produced an income distribution not nearly so unequally divided. The primary consideration is that wealth distribution in 1870 may be used to estimate saving distribution in 1870. This result, in turn, may be employed to characterize an income curve for 1870 that seems to be realistic.

Distribution of Consumption

Tocqueville stressed in the 1830s that America had "equality of condition," which meant that men lived in the same manner, indulged in the same pleasures, and frequented the same places. How could this condition have existed if wealth was so unevenly distributed as we found it to be in 1850? It existed because Tocqueville was speaking of equality of consumption and not of wealth. The model described above shows the top percentile in income distribution to have 15 percent of total income and 12 percent of total consumption. These figures are far less than the 27-30 percent share of wealth held by the top 1 percent of wealthholders at midcentury. We do not wish to suggest that a group consuming 12 times as much as an average group is living in a moderate fashion. America still had Natchez and Newport but it did not have Tocqueville's chateaux of the Loire Valley or a Versailles.[40]

Summary

We have investigated in this chapter the shares of wealth held by the rich, the near-rich, and middle-wealth groups in the

United States at midcentury. We have determined that the
rich held surprisingly large portions of wealth as early as
1850. The top 1 percent of realholders owned 30 and 29
percent of real estate, respectively, in 1850 and 1860, and
the top 1 percent of wealthholders owned 29 and 27 percent of total estate in 1860 and 1870. Lampman's figures
for this group are 32 percent for 1922 and 25 percent in
1953. Perhaps the share in 1962-63 was 29 percent.

General inequality for all men in 1870 was very similar
to that for free men in 1860 as measured by Lorenz curves
and Gini coefficients. Inequality in the decade remained
constant in the North but decreased among whites in the
South to the level in the North, primarily because of the
destruction of slave values of the former southern plutocracy. The addition of former slaves to the population
brought southern inequality back above its former level.
The inequality coefficient for the United States was closer
to that of the North in 1870 than in 1860 because, relatively, there was so much more wealth in the North in 1870.
The Gini coefficient for the United States was .83 for free
men in 1860, .81 for whites in 1870, and .83 for all men
in 1870.

The available evidence indicates that inequality of wealth
remained the same from 1800 to 1940 and then decreased
a little, particularly among middle-wealth groups. This conclusion is based on the censuses of wealth of 1850-70,
censuses of mortgages from 1880 to 1889, a census of farm
and homeowners of 1890, tax appraisals for Indiana from
1870 to 1900 and Kentucky in 1800, slave distributions
from 1790 to 1860, and United States inheritance and income tax data since 1914. A plutocratic elite emerged at
the turn of the century but it did not fundamentally alter
the share of wealth held by the top 1 percent of persons.
The main point is that there already was strong inequality
in 1860, 1870, and earlier.

5. Land and Slave Inequality

We have studied the inequality of wealth ownership among men up to this point only in terms of dollar values. The physical quantities involved in these values—land acreage, lots, homes, rooms in homes, slaves, horses, livestock, stores factories, and so on—are important items that convey separa facets of the historical change in inequality. In this chapter, two of these measures, land acreage and slaves, will be single out because they were such crucial quantities in the determi nation of average wealth and its relative dispersion in the agricultural sector. Furthermore, there are excellent statistic figures available for acreage and slaves, not only at mid-century but also from 1790 in the case of slaves, and, for a longer overview, up to the present in the case of farm acreage. The broad area of agriculture will be understood more clearly from the viewpoint of farming as an occupatio the seemingly inevitable inequality of wealth among farmer: will be clarified by a study such as this, which helps to tie dollar values more closely to the lives of people.

Why the United States had as much inequality as it did at midcentury is an exceedingly difficult question to answer. Only about 5 percent of the total variation in total estate is explained by age, occupation, nativity, residence, and color as we have measured them, and it is doubtful if significant measurable variables could be found to explain more than another 10 percent of the variation in total estate. Correlations, including detailed information on ethnicity and religion, have explained 12 percent of the variation for certain formulations in Canada in 1871. Inherited wealth undoubtedly would contribute to our understanding but there is always the gnawing question of how the inequality of inheritance arose. The subject of inequality is further complicated because there is general lack of agreement on whetl the United States either has now, or had in the past, an important problem in the maldistribution of wealth. The gamut of views of nineteenth-century writers included Tocqueville, who was obsessed with the tyranny caused by equality of condition, and Frederick Olmstead, who was describing in detail the inequality in condition of whites and slaves in the South.[1] Later in the century Turner presented yet another interpretation when he almost romanticized equality of condition on the frontier:

> The wilderness masters the colonist. It finds him a European in dress, industries, tools, modes of travel, and thought. It takes him from the railroad car and puts him in the birch canoe. It strips off the garments of civilization and arrays him in the hunting shirt and the moccasin.[2]

We can provide some links between the dollar values of real and personal estate and the lives of people by studying the statistics on the inequality of land and of slavery at midcentury. One is then better able to judge how much inequality actually existed.

Farm Acreage

It behooves us to examine data from the censuses of agriculture to obtain an understanding of the distribution of real estate at midcentury. Frequency tables of the size of farms in the North and South before and after the Civil War give valuable clues about the changes in inequality that took place at that period. It is also fruitful to study inequality in size of farms through time by considering each decennial census up to the present. The resulting frequency tables on acreage are the best continuous series measure in the United States of the unequal economic condition of a large group of people.

1850 Distribution

Census officials unfortunately did not publish the results of tabulations of farm size in 1850. The only distribution is a sample of counties chosen from seven states. Let us briefly examine its frequency table, neglecting farms of less than 10 acres.

Published-census sample from 7 states in 1850

A Lower class limit (improved acres)	$100N_A$ Percentage of farmers above A
1,000	.34
100	12.55
50	26.23
10	100.00

Source: Compendium 1850, pp. 153, 175, 191. The states were Kentucky, Michigan, Pennsylvania, Rhode Island, South Carolina, Louisiana and Ohio. The sample size was 23,325.

Farmers in the spin sample who were propertyholders from these same states (but not restricted to any particular counties in the states) have been pooled to obtain some semblance of real estate values from the same areas. I decided to examine only those farmers with $100 or more in real estate. I arrived at this limit by considering the minimum 10-acre limit and the fact that at that time the average cash value of farms was $11.42 per acre of improved land in the United States. The informal table shows the results.

Spin sample of the 7 states in 1850

RE Lower real estate class limit	$100N_{RE}$ Percentage of farmers above RE
$10,000	.1
1,000	12.0
500	26.8
100	100.0

Note that there are about the same proportions of farmers

above each real estate value, RE, as there are 10 times the amount of acreage, 10A. Thus, 26.2 percent of farms were 50 or more acres in size and 26.8 percent of farmers had $500 or more in real estate. This suggests that land acreage distribution and real estate valuation were similar.

1860 Distribution

We can be more confident with 1860 values because tabulations of farm size taking into account the number of improved acres were made for the entire country. The figures, shown in table 5.1, allow a much more sophisticated analysis. Given the proportion of farms, N_A, above a given

Table 5.1. Size of Farms Related to Size of Real Estate

Census of farm size for farms of 3 or more improved acres in 1860			*Spin sample of farmers having real estate in 1860*		
A	*(Number of farms in the interval A)*	*$100N_A$*	*$100N_{RE}$ (forced to equal N_A)*	*RE (interpolated at N_{RE})*	*RE/A*
1,000	5,364	.27	.27	$50,000	$50/acre
500	20,319	1.3	1.3	25,000	50
100	487,041	26.2	26.2	3,300	33
50	608,878	57.4	57.4	1,200	24
20	616,558	88.9	88.9	360	18
10	162,178	97.2	97.2	150	15
3	54,676	100.0	100.0	1	
	1,955,014				

Sources: Spin samples of 1860 and U.S. Census Office, 8th Census, 1860, *Agriculture of the United States in 1860*, p. 247.

acreage A, we can search for an equivalent, $N_{RE} = N_A$, in the real estate distribution. An example from the table shows .275 percent of farms greater than 1,000 acres; search in the upper cumulated real estate distribution to the point where the proportion of farmers is also approximately .275 percent and note that this is a group above $50,000 in real

estate. Comparison of the A value of 1,000 acres with
$50,000 implies that most of these very rich farmers do in
fact own these very large farms. The assertion is a bold one,
but we know that there was remarkable similarity between
farm cash value reported in the farm schedule of the census
manuscripts and real estate that was reported in the population schedule.

The various values of A and RE, obtained by letting N_A =
N_{RE}, are plotted in chart 5.1. Note that the regression equation for the six points is RE = $8.10 A^{1.28}$ for propertyholding farmers and size of farms. Significantly, the elasticity
coefficient of 1.28 is greater than 1. The larger farms presumably have higher value per acre and/or persons with great
wealth have more than one farm. Thus land distribution is
not a perfect guide to wealth distribution because there is a
magnification factor. A farm 10 percent larger than another
has perhaps 12.8 percent greater value, or better, is associated
with an individual having 12.8 percent more value of real
estate. It is somewhat difficult to compute the concentration
coefficient G for acreage because of the assumption that we
must make about midpoints of classes; one calculation[3]
gives G = .44 for acres in 1860. The 1860 real estate coefficient of .62 for propertyholder farmers means that this
general measure of inequality is one-third larger than that
of land. Even this significant increase does not include the
effect of propertyless farmers. The coefficient for 1860 real
estate of all farmers is .78. The inequality in the distribution
of real estate value among all farmers was substantially larger
than the inequality in the size of farms. I state briefly in
summary the inequality coefficients of land acreage of farms
and the value of real estate among propertied farmers and all
farmers in the accompanying table. The inequality levels
remained fixed before and after the war.

The fact that inequality of real estate is so large relative to
that of acreage should not lead the reader to minimize the
importance of land inequality, particularly that stemming

Chart 5.1. Indirect Relationship, Using Cumulative Curves for the United States in 1860, of Size of Farms and Average Real Estate Holdings of Male Farmers 20 and Older Who Reported Property

RE or real estate
holdings in dollars

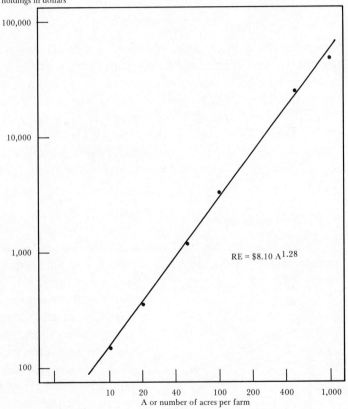

$$RE = \$8.10 \, A^{1.28}$$

A or number of acres per farm

Source: See table 5.1.

Notes: Let N_A be the proportion of farms larger than acreage A and N_{RE} be the proportion of farm propertyholders above real estate value RE. Values of A and RE are generated by equating N_A and N_{RE}.

| | *Gini coefficients of* | | |
	Farm acres	*RE of propertied*	*RE of all*
1850 free	?	.61	.77
1860 free	.45	.62	.78
1870 whites		.59	.76
1870 all	.46	.59	.79
1880 all	.45	—	—

from the many small farms. Not everyone had 160 acres or
even 80 acres of improved land by any stretch of the imagina-
tion. The average number of improved acres per farm in 1860
was only 83, and the majority of farms were smaller than
the mean. For farms of 3 or more acres, only 26 percent
were over 100 acres and 57 percent over 50 acres. There was
a marked lower tail of the distribution, which implies that
almost half the farmers had less acreage than they might
have wished to own.

Pareto Implications

We can measure this land deficiency by the gap between
the inverse Pareto straight line showing constant inequality
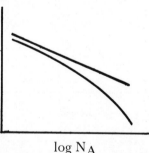 above any given acreage
figure and the actual
parabolic inverse Pareto
curve. It was found that
the four frequency classes
above 50 acres in table 5.1
conform rather closely to
the straight-line pattern of
the inverse Pareto curve.
This straight line, with its
slope of .55, may be projected to imply that the smallest
farm should be at least 42 acres in size. In this case the inequality level prevailing above 50 acres would also prevail
below 50 acres to a value of 42 acres. The frequency curve

would have a reverse J shape with no lower tail. It would have necessitated 12 percent more acres of improved land than existed at the time to eliminate the lower tail. The straight-line portion above 50 acres could be projected farther to the point that would include all 3.51 million farmers and farm laborers in 1860. This number was 1.79 times the number of farms above 3 acres. The projection results suggest that all farms would be larger than 21 acres and would necessitate aggregate improved acreage 46 percent larger than actually existed.[4] This can only mean that all farmers were not landowners in America and that the many who were landowners had less than 50 acres of improved land. A methodical projection based on the inequality above 50 acres leads to the conclusion that it would have been necessary to have 50 percent more land in order to accommodate all those desiring to own land.

The idea that men could have land only for the asking must definitely be qualified. Amasa Walker wrote in 1866 that "Land here is so cheap, labor so much in demand, that no able bodied man has any excuse for pauperism."[5] This statement does not adequately explain why there were so many farmers without much improved land or any land at all, or why middle classes did not have more wealth relative to upper classes in a nation with such abundance. It was more than a problem of aging or nativity among middle classes since each of these subsets had a relative absence of wealth. Perhaps information on land accumulation for a family over a period of three, four, or five generations might explain a significant part of the variation in holdings. One Pennsylvania pamphleteer wrote in 1776 that sizable wealth was "unavoidable to the descendants of the early settlers" and thus that wealth of the rich rose in an accidental fashion and was not based on the activities of the individual.[6]

Farmland Inequality, 1860–1964

The distribution of farm sizes is about the only distribution

series that has been gathered on any continuing basis from
1860 to the present. Inequality coefficients may be computed for the decennial censuses to 1950 and for the agricultural censuses of 1959 and 1964. Because the number of
farms is small today, the figures are probably of little value
in depicting inequality of wealth since at least the 1930s.
They are of great interest, however, in the interval from
1860 to 1910 as indicators of change in relative wealthholdings.

One major problem with the statistics stems from the
distinction between unimproved and crop and grazing land.
As the country developed, noncrop farms of huge size appeared in the West and Southwest so that distributions
using only farm size can be misleading. It is of merit to
limit our analysis to the 21 states of the northern census
regions of the New England, Middle Atlantic, and North
Central areas. Measures are given in table 5.2 with several

Table 5.2. Farmland Inequality in Northern Census Regions of the
United States from 1860 to 1964 Using the Gini Coefficient (G) and the Inverse Pareto Slope (B)

	G	B		G	B
1860	.44^{xy}	.38	1920	.41	.48
1870	.42^{xy}	.36	1930	.41	.48
1880	.37^{x}	.39	1940	.46	.53
1890	.36^{x}	.38	1950	.47	.56
1900	.40^{x}	.45	1959	.47	.58
1910	.40	.41	1964	.49	.59

Sources: Censuses of Agriculture, various years. The slope B is calculated considering the number above 500 and 1,000 acres.

Note: x = improved acreage only; y = calculated from assumed midpoints (see n. 7).

qualifications.[7] The 1860 and 1870 values are for improved
land only. Unfortunately this concept was not continued
for size distributions after these dates; the later-year values
are probably not comparable with them. Nevertheless, one

can agree that farm-size inequality remained relatively constant from 1860 to 1910 or 1920 in the northern states. There is certainly no indication that it had a long cycle. I admit that the data do not measure multiple farmholdings or tenancy.

The inverse Pareto slopes for the sizes of all farms in the country might properly be examined for the top tail of the distribution. These slopes, measured only between the class 1,000 acres and up and 500 acres, are .53 in 1860, .42 in 1870, .53 in 1880, .54 in 1890, .60 in 1900, and .55 in 1910. I believe that the drop in 1870 was quite real and reflected the state of affairs in the South after the Civil War. Otherwise it seems that inequality was fairly constant for 50 years.

There is no doubt that large farms in the South dominated real estate distribution. Of the 5,364 farms of 1,000 acres or more reported in the 1860 census, 4,572 were in the South. Substantial differences also appear for farms of 500 and more acres. In dollar value terms, the top 1 percent in 1850 held 28 percent of real estate for those in the North and 35 percent for those in the South. Whether land fertility made large slaveholdings feasible or, conversely, large slaveholdings made large landholdings feasible is another question. The interesting fact is that the southern inequality coefficient of real estate value of .875 is so great that it almost matches that of real estate holdings of urban (nonfarm) persons in the North in 1870. It was as large as the coefficient for total estate of urban persons in the North in 1870. All these statements are evidence of great inequality in this country.[8]

Slave Distribution in 1860

We shall now examine southern personal estate by concentrating on the distribution of slaves. There is no question about the fact that the difference in wealth of freemen in the North

and South before the war could be attributed almost entirely to slave values. If one could eliminate slave market value
from the distribution of wealth in the South in 1860, he
could see that the inequality levels in the North and South
were similar. It should be possible to construct a synthetic
distribution for the South in 1860 that would be very
similar to the southern distribution for whites in 1870.
This can be done by eliminating slave values and by including nonwhites in the lower tail of the wealth curve.

Distribution of Slaves among Slaveholders

It is fortunate that the census authorities tabulated the
number of slaves held by each slaveholder in 1860. These
detailed data are presented in chart 5.2 and in abridged
form in table 5.3. The average number of slaves was 10.3

Table 5.3. Distribution of Slaves among Slaveholders in the South in
1860 and Upper-Tail Counterparts from the Distributions
of Personal and Total Estate in the South in 1860

Distribution of slaves			Spin-sample counterparts		
SL, number of slaves owned	Cumulative number of slaveholders in class		*(interpolated at $N_{SL} = N_{PE} = N_{TE}$)*		
(lower class limit)	Number	Percentage, $100N_{SL}$	PE	PE/SL	TE
1,000	1	.00005			
500	14	.00070	$619,000	$1,400	$957,000
100	2,292	.115	100,000	1,000	160,000
50	10,659	.536	50,000	1,000	72,000
10	107,992	5.43	10,000	1,000	17,200
5	197,548	9.93	4,750	950	8,800
1	384,884	19.3	1,500	1,500	3,670
0	1,990,000	100.	0		0

Sources: Agriculture Census, 1860, p. 247; and spin sample of 1860.

for the 384,884 slaveholders in the South. We can approximate the number of nonslaveholders as the number necessary

Chart 5.2. Inverse Pareto Curves of Slaves and Total and Personal Estate among Adult Free
    Males in the South in 1860

X, total estate in
thousands of dollars
or number of slaves

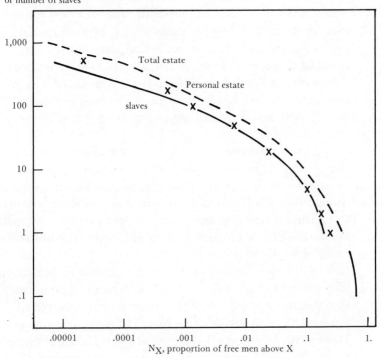

Source: See table 5.3.

to bring this total to 1.99 million adult free males. There is solid evidence of a decreasing span of control. The ratio of the number of slaveholders with 100 or more slaves to the number with 10 or more slaves is far less than the ratio of the number with 10 or more to those with 1 or more. This Pareto parabola shown in chart 5.2 shows only 1 slave-holder with more than 1,000 slaves. Some law of diminishing returns in slave management must have been present for large groups of slaves. One would need overseers of overseers, necessitating some sort of corporate structure that did not exist in the South. Land requirements presented spatial problems, and overseers of individual plantations were changed frequently. Thus, the inequality of slaveholdings among slaveholders, G = .62, was not exorbitant.[9] The great inequality factor, that 80 percent of freemen had zero wealth in slaves, increased inequality from .62 to the very high value of .93.

There is a strong relationship between southern inequality and wealth inequality, as shown by the cumulative distributions of chart 5.2. The graphic similarity makes it appear as though slave distribution itself forced wealth distribution to be what it was. We can achieve greater precision by matching slaves (SL) and personal estate (PE) using the more than cumulative distributions (N_{SL} and N_{PE}). Chart 5.2 shows that the proportion of top men is the same in each distribution when PE = $1,000 SL. Thus, .1 percent of men have 100 slaves or more and $100,000 or more of personal estate. The same relationship holds when N_{SL} and N_{PE} are 1 percent or 10 percent. It appears that personal estate distribution between the top .1 percent and the top 10 percent is definitely molded by the slave figures. Exact interpolations yield a ratio of personal estate to number of slaves of $917 to $1,000 at all 16 available class limits from 3 to 200 slaves.

The personal distribution might have been duplicated exactly by the slave distribution if units had been less than integers. It is possible to duplicate the inequality coefficient

for total estate fairly well by knowing the details of the
slaveholder distribution and assuming that all wealthholders
had .5 of a slave more than they did. There is an important
deviation from $1,000 per slave in the case of 1 and 2
slaves. A regression equation fitted to personal estate points
between 1 and 9 slaves produces PE = $461 + $890 SL.
This equation is not swamped by the very large values and
indicates that slaves were closer to $900, with an intercept
cash equivalent of perhaps half a slave.

Distribution and Valuation of Slaves in Counties

Information about slaves and valuation of slaves was
given in the 1860 census for 1,105 counties in the South.
The number of slaveholders and slaves was reported for
1,088 of these counties. The aggregate dollar valuation of
personal estate of freemen, mostly dominated by slave valua-
tions, was also given by county. We can isolate the effect of
slaves on personal estate from these data. Table 5.4 shows
that there is an extremely methodical increase in the average
wealth as one goes up the ladder from one slave class to another, using a class interval of one slave.[10] The plotting of
this relationship, given in chart 5.3, reveals that the highest
of the 13 slave classes is out of line. This is due to the con-
fusion arising from the fact that 16 counties in Louisiana
classified slaves, at least in part, as real estate instead of
personal estate.[11] If we fit a least-squares regression equation to the 12 classes from 0 to 14 slaves per adult freeman
(afree), we have: Personal estate/afree + $598 + $911
slaves/afree. There is good reason to use $900 as the proper
valuation for slaves.[12]

The rounded-value equation of PE/afree = $600 + $900
SL/afree is attractive. The intercept of $600 is an estimate
of average personal estate in a county in the South if it had
no slaves. This figure really does not differ materially from
the average personal estate in the North in 1860 of $660.

Chart 5.3. Relationship between Personal Estate and Number of Slaves for 1,105 Southern Counties in 1860

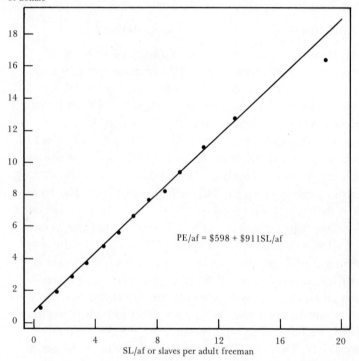

PE/af or personal
estate per adult
freeman in thousands
of dollars

PE/af = $598 + $911SL/af

SL/af or slaves per adult freeman

Source: See table 6.3. The 1,105 have been distributed among 13 slave classes.

Table 5.4. Personal Estate Classified by Slaveholdings for Each of
1,105 Counties in the South in 1860

Slaves per adult freeman (class limits)		Number of counties	Personal estate average[a]
0–	.99	463	$ 940
1–	1.99	187	1,890
2–	2.99	135	2,960
3–	3.99	82	3,750
4–	4.99	67	4,670
5–	5.99	48	5,650
6–	6.99	32	6,680
7–	7.99	19	7,590
8–	8.99	18	8,200
9–	9.99	16	9,440
10–	11.99	18	10,970
12–	13.99	8	12,800
14 and up		12	16,300
All		1,105	2,928

Sources: Population Census, 1860, pp. 2-592, for obtaining the number of freemen and slaves; *Mortality and Miscellaneous Statistics, 1860,* table 3, pp. 296-319, for obtaining the aggregate wealth in personal estate in each county.

[a]See n. 10.

The slope of $900 might be $1,000 if one considered slaves as a proxy also for nonslave PE in cash, inventories, livestock, furniture, and so on. Observe that the rounded-value equation is similar to those of the preceding section for men with 10 or fewer slaves.

The ratio of the price of slaves to the price of land in the South in 1860 was about 1/26. This comes from our slave estimate of $900 and average cash value of farm acreage of $34.30. This ratio would signify that a proper production function with land and slaves as independent variables would reveal marginal productivities in the same ratio. Some evidence exists from the county data, arranged by slaves per freeman, that an additional slave is associated with 25-30 more acres of land per freeman. This is indirect verification of the prices listed above. The distribution of total estate of farmers in the South in 1860 might be fairly well duplicated, at least relatively, by multiplying each farmer's acreage by $34 and his slaves by $900.

Anticipating Post-Emancipation Distribution

An approximation of wealth inequality for whites in the South in 1870 could be made by subtracting slave value at each percentile of the distribution of 1860 total estate. We can see this in chart 5.2, which gives the inverse Pareto curves for total estate and slaves. Suppose we multiply that slave curve by $900 and subtract it from the total estate curve. The result should be an approximation of the relative Pareto curve for 1870 whites except for a discontinuity among wealthholders without slaves in the percentile range just below the top 20 percent. Statistics necessary for making the computation are given in table 5.3, and the projected curve matches the actual curve rather closely in general shape below $50,000. Some examples not corrected for price change are given in the informal table.

PE in 1870	Proportion of men, N_{PE}	
	Projected	*Actual*
$50,000	.0022	.0039
20,000	.013	.015
10,000	.040	.042
5,000	.090	.095
2,770	.193	.162
1,000	.379	.330

Distribution of Personal Estate in 1870

Average personal estate in the South for whites fell dramatically from $2,195 in 1860 to $649 in 1870.[13] These two figures and their difference of $1,546 may be fortuitous but I tend to believe otherwise. One immediately thinks of

$1,800, or the product of two slaves at $900 per slave. The $649 is also very similar to the $660 average in the North in 1860. A statistical nicety is achieved by cutting the $649 by the price deflator of 1.41. This gives a value of $460 and a difference of $2,195-$460, or $1,735; this is closer to a $900 mean for two slaves.

The accompanying table gives summary information concerning inequality levels of personal estate.

	G_{PE}		
	1860 free	1870 whites	1870 all
South	.87	.79	.84
North	.83	.85	.85
United States	.87	.84	.85

Amazingly, inequality of personal estate remained fairly constant in the South; decreased inequality associated with elimination of slave values was counterbalanced by the addition of emancipated Negroes. There was a crossing of the Lorenz curves for free men in the South in 1860 and 1870. It can be noted that inequality of personal estate of the free was similar in the South and the United States and, indeed, similar to the Gini values for real and total estate.

Slave Distribution before 1860

We have established that slavery was a significant part of southern wealth in 1860. The inequality level of slaves was similar to that of overall wealth inequality among individuals in the South because personal estate was such a large part of total estate. How great was slave inequality in earlier periods? In 1850? In 1790? If answers to these questions can be found, one may make strong inferences about wealth distribution back to 1790, at least in the South. If there had been any census of total wealth prior to 1860, one could have studied the North as well as the South. The best information is limited to slaveholdings.

1850 Distribution

There is evidence of a slight increase in the concentration of ownership of slaves in the period from 1850 to 1860. The ratio of the number of slaveholders to the number of adult freemen in the South was .232 in 1850 and .194 in 1860. The number of slaves per slaveholder was higher in 1860 than in 1850 whereas the number of slaves per adult male was lower. Some of these differences are subject to measurement error. Perhaps the census tabulators did a better job in 1860 in combining multifarm and multiplantation holdings of one owner. The author knows from working with slave data in a few southern counties that one man might have slaves listed in many places in a county. In any case, the figures in table 5.5 indicate considerable consistency.[14] I believe they are strong enough to build the

Table 5.5. Distribution of Slaves among Slaveholders in the South in 1850 and 1860

Number of slaves	*Number of slaveholders in class*	
(lower class limit)	*1850*	*1860*
1,000	2	1
500	9	13
100	1,722	2,278
50	6,196	8,367
10	84,328	97,333
5	80,765	89,556
1	174,503	187,336
0	1,152,475	1,605,116
	1,500,000	1,990,000

Sources: Compendium, 1850, pp. 94-95; see also table 5.3.

argument that the distribution of personal estate remained essentially constant from 1850 to 1860 in the United States. In 1860, 56 percent of the aggregate personal estate in the United States was reported by persons in the South; the ratio of slave valuation to aggregate personal estate was

$3.6 billion to $7.7 billion, or 46 percent. Slave valuation
and southern valuation must have been a very important
part of the total in 1850. Frederick Olmstead characterized
the southern hierarchy in 1854 as follows:

> The wealth class is the commanding class in most
> districts of the South, and gives character to all the
> slaveholding class. Wealth is less distributed, and is more
> retained in families at the South than the North. With
> the slaveholding class there is a pride of birth and social
> position, much more than in any class at the North. This
> affects the character and conduct of individuals . . . and
> on the whole community.[15]

We can observe in table 5.5 that the top .1 percent of men in
the South, a group constituting 1,700-2,300 individuals, was
in this commanding class with 100 or more slaves each.

1790 and 1830 Distributions

I have taken a sample of 14 southern states and the District
of Columbia from the census manuscript film for 1830 and
have determined that the relative distribution of slaves among
slaveholders was almost exactly the same in that year as it
was in 1850 for the same southern states.[16] Distributions of
slaveholdings derived from the 1790 census have been published for the states of South Carolina, North Carolina,
Maryland, and the District of Columbia. These distributions
account for about half the slaves in the South at that time.
It is determined that the relative inequality of the distribution of slaves among slaveholders in these four areas was
almost the same in the years 1790, 1830, 1850, and 1860.[17]

The author early became interested in Mississippi because
it had an increased number of slaves per freeman, averaging
1.1 percent a year from 1800 to 1860. Its average number
of slaves in 1860 was the highest in the South except for
South Carolina. Its G values for slaves among adult free in
1830, 1840, and 1860 were, respectively, .86, .87, and .86,

and for slaves among slaveholders in the same years they were .59, .61, and .61. Adams County, Mississippi, is attractive as a study because it includes Natchez and is part of the Mississippi Delta region of slavery. Results for 1802 and 1810, using poll tax data, and for 1830, 1840, and 1860, using United States data, show excellent constancy of slave inequality in this country.

Age and Slave Wealth in 1800

Data for adult age were first obtained in the 1800 census for three broad classes. Studies of the ages of slaveholders in 1800 in five southern states and New York were reported initially in chapter 2. We could now add further detail by describing the average number of slaves of age-specific slaveholder classes. The results are that slaves were an excellent proxy for wealth in 1800 and that age-slave patterns in 1800 are similar to age–wealth patterns of 1860. It seems that the age–wealth cycle was very evident at the birth of the country.

Wealth of Nonwhites in 1870

The emerging freedom of nonwhites already had some impact on wealth figures by 1870. These data are particularly intriguing because they are an incipient form of the data for whites. Table 5.6 provides evidence that their inequality levels were strangely similar in the sense that a few held wealth. We see summary measures for the two groups in the informal table. One could also demonstrate that the

	Mean	Inequality coefficient	Population (millions)
Nonwhites	$ 74	.908	1.08
Whites	2,691	.814	8.69

accumulation rates are alike in terms of age-specific wealth

Table 5.6. Proportion of Adult Males with Total Estates above Stated
Levels (N_{TE}) for Nonwhites and Whites in 1870

Total estate (lower class limit)	Nonwhites $100N_{TE}$	Whites $100N_{TE}$
$ 0	100.0	100.0
1	20.4	62.0
100	19.0	61.4
200	10.5	57.1
500	3.9	47.2
1,000	1.6	37.7
2,000	.5	27.1
5,000	.0	13.8

Source: Spin sample.

averages. The ratio of mean white wealth to mean nonwhite
wealth was roughly constant for the five age classes from 20
to 69, but the gradient for nonwhites is not so steep at this
early stage of freedom.

It is possible to compare the position of nonwhites in
1962 with the positions of nonwhites and whites in 1870.
Wealth levels for nonwhites have grown very substantially at
an annual rate of 3.0 percent a year. Yet the nonwhite
average is still far below that of whites. Even more shocking,
perhaps, is that average wealth for nonwhites today is less
than that of whites in 1870. Nonwhite wealth in 1962, corrected for changes in prices and changes in age composition,
was only 40 percent of white wealth in 1870.[18]

Summary

We have determined that the frequency table for the size of
farms had decidedly less relative dispersion than did wealth
in real estate but that there was a pronounced lower tail of
farms with little improved acreage. Thus, middle-wealth
groups really held very little wealth in America. Inequality
of farm size seems to have remained constant since 1850.

The extreme inequality in distribution of slaves among slaveholders in the South caused a great deal of general inequality even among whites. A projection of southern wealth inequality for 1870, made by subtracting the estimated value of slaves from wealth distribution in 1860, proved to be quite successful. Wealth among nonwhites in 1870 was at a very low level but its relative spread was similar to that for whites. Inequality coefficients of frequency tables for slaveholders, classified by number of slaves, were similar from 1790 to 1860. Thus, the two major institutions in America that determined inequality, outside the manufacturing and the industrial arenas, were responsible for gross inequities. Land inequality as manifested in real estate values and slave inequality as ramified in personal estate values made agrarian America a land of unevenly distributed resources.

6. Wealth, Origin, and Residence in 1860

A special effort was made to study the area of birth of the men drawn in the 1860 sample. I shall single out those listing their place of birth as England, Scotland, Ireland, and Germany among our foreign born and those listing birth in New England, the South, and Ohio and west among our native born. I wish to quantify how much more the English had accumulated than the Germans, how much more the Germans had accumulated than the Irish, and whether wealth of Yankees varied according to where they were born in New England. An interesting aspect of birth classifications arises when they are cross classified by areas of residence, particularly the Northeast and Northwest.

A fresh approach to the characteristics of wealth can be gathered from the aggregate wealth figures for counties in 1860, which, fortunately, were published. I made a study of 2,068 counties, 963 in the North and 1,105 in the South. I will report cross-classification tables and regression equations that treat such factors as population density, location, wages, extent of manufacturing, and improved acreage. The richest counties in the country are identified. A special sample was drawn from the county with the highest average and a few aspects of its individuals are given.

Areas of Birth

Results obtained from classifying men in the 1860 spin sample by country or state of birth will be described. A partial analysis found that patterns in 1870 were most often the same as those in 1860, so they need not be presented. Examples of similarities are that English living in the Northeast had more wealth than English living in the Northwest in both years, while Irish fared better in the Northwest in

both years. As a contrast there were fewer persons of southern birth living in the North in 1870 than in 1860.

Men born in the United States were much more likely to
have had native-born parents than foreign-born parents. This
follows from the fact that only 18 percent of white men
were foreign born in 1850 (26 and 28 percent, respectively,
in 1860 and 1870). If it were assumed that the proportion
of adult males who were foreign born remained constant at
.20 and that family sizes were similar among nativity groups,
the probability might be about .80 that a native-born person
had a native-born father, $.8^2$ (or .64) that his grandfather
was born in the United States, and $.8^3$ (or .51) that his great-
grandfather was born in the United States. Thus, perhaps
half the native born could trace their paternal line to as
many as three generations in America.

This advantage of three generations of American growth
could easily explain why the wealth average of native-born
whites was 1.5-2.5 times that of the foreign born. It is even
possible to construct a theoretical distribution from the
above probabilities and generation differentials in wealth
that shows the relative inequality of the actual wealth
distribution. The implication would be that a man whose
ancestors had been in the United States one generation
longer than another would have expected somewhat more
wealth. He would inherit not only a larger estate but also
probably greater economic opportunity and business
acumen. The model could easily be adapted to the fact
that roughly one-third of native born had not been able
to accumulate at a given census date.

It will be shown that natives born in certain New England
states seemed to excel in wealth aggrandizement no matter
where they lived in the United States. Such individuals were
born in states that included New York and Massachusetts,
as contrasted with those born in Ohio. There is the implication that these Yankees were more likely to have had
ancestors with American experience and heritage. However,

I cannot prove this, particularly since the proportion of foreign born was about the same in the Northwest and Northeast around 1850 to 1860.

Characteristics of Nativity Groups

The data of table 6.1 teem with interesting patterns for 1860. Suppose an individual were native born; knowledge

Table 6.1. Characteristics of Males 20 and Older Living in the United States in 1860 Classified by Country, State, or Region of Birth

Country, state, or region of birth (but not necessarily of residence)	Characteristic						
	N	$\overline{TE}$	G_{TE}	$\overline{Age}$	$\overline{nA}$	$\overline{So}$	$\overline{TE}_{No}$
1. Me., N.H., Vt.	.06	$2,580	.787	40.4	.503	.05	$2,398
2. Conn., Mass., R.I.	.07	3,417	.822	41.4	.619	.08	3,351
3. N.Y., N.J.	.15	2,926	.811	38.0	.492	.04	2,738
4. Pa.	.09	2,348	.728	39.0	.499	.06	2,340
5. Ohio	.06	1,625	.780	31.8	.366	.06	1,511
6. Ind., Ill., Mich.	.03	1,192	.783	29.5	.363	.10	1,146
7. Southern states	.28	3,879	.828	38.2	.368	.77	2,484
8. Northern states	.47	2,524	.807	37.6	.489	.06	2,417
9. Native born	.74	3,027	.816	37.8	.444	.32	2,425
10. England, Scotland, Wales	.04	1,822	.834	38.4	.580	.12	1,555
11. Holland, Switzerland, Scandinavia	.01	1,442	.844	36.9	.576	.17	1,506
12. Germany	.09	1,247	.807	37.0	.663	.18	1,209
13. Ireland	.09	1,021	.897	36.3	.747	.13	965
14. Foreign born	.26	1,297	.858	36.8	.682	.15	1,161
15. Others	.04	1,315	.883	35.0	.642	.14	1,038
16. Total persons	1.00	2,580	.832	37.5	.506	.28	2,040

Source: Spin sample of 13,696 from schedule 1 of the 1860 census.

Note: N = proportion of total population; $\overline{TE}$ = average total estate; G_{TE} = Gini coefficient; $\overline{age}$ = average age; $\overline{nA}$ = proportion non-farmer; $\overline{So}$ = proportion living in South; $\overline{TE}_{No}$ = average wealth of those living in the North.

of his region of birth reveals several things, as shown in the first six columns of the table. The longitudinal vector from west to east is associated with age, urbanity, and higher wealth. It is possible to calculate that this greater eastern wealth is explained only in part by older age. A least-squares line fitted to TE and age for the six points of the first six regions shows that those of a given age had 6.1 percent more mean wealth than the group one year younger.[1] This is a substantially larger gradient than we are accustomed to for the country as a whole.[2] The younger man born in Illinois is not accumulating so much as we would have expected had there been no differences attributable to birth area within the native-born group. The older man born in Massachusetts accumulates more than we would have expected. There is a premium for being a Yankee.

The foreign-born figures add a new dimension to our analysis. We need not be bothered very much with the relatively small differences of ages among each of the regions 10, 11, 12, and 13 of table 6.1. Those born in England, Scotland, and Wales have an average of about $1,800, those of Germany have one of $1,200, and those of Ireland $1,000. Individuals from Holland, Switzerland, and Scandinavia at $1,400 are within this range. These data are crude because of a confounding effect from slave values. (Average wealth for those living in the North is given in the last column of the table.) Nevertheless, the largely urban Irish were at a level one-half to two-thirds of the English. They, in turn, were at a level one-half to two-thirds of those born in the northern states. One can only make conjectures about these disparities. Do they reflect the cultural and economic differences of the countries from which the individuals come? They could. It is known, for example, that the number of rooms per person in Glasgow was two-thirds the number in Edinburgh in 1861. The numbers in some of the poorer counties of Scotland were half those of the more affluent.[3] How could one expect other than that the Irish average would be half that of the English?

It seems natural to expect differences in wealth among native born classified by area of birth even though these differences might not be so spectacular as they are for foreign born. Is it not true that the individual with a Yankee heritage should have an advantage? Yes, but the individual born in Illinois may have been the son of a dynamic Yankee who moved west at a very early date, earlier than 1840 or 1830 if the son is of average age in 1860. Average wealth values by region of birth in the United States are listed in table 6.1. Averages for those born in the East are substantially higher than for those born in the West. Unfortunately, these figures are strongly affected by the fact that average age of men born in Ohio and farther west was about 10 years less than that of men born in the East. We must standardize our wealth for age of men and also for whether or not they resided in slave areas.

Standardized Wealth Values

Wealth averages by area of birth are given in table 6.2 after correcting or standardizing for age differences and residence differences.[4] It is considered a fair representation of average wealth if the ages of individuals were the same for each birth group and if the same proportions of men in each birth group were living in the North and South [in the case of cols. (1) and (2) of table 6.2]. We proceed to comment on results.

The actual United States figures for nativity groups are influenced by some differences in southern residence and even more by differences in age. The column labeled (1) shows that adjustment for slave residence and age still leaves a clear east–west gradient. The Yankee-born average was 30 percent larger than that for Ohio born and 50 percent larger than that for those born in region 6 (Ind., Ill., Mich.). This disparity is not so great as the 60 percent differential between British and Irish born but it is significant nevertheless. Perhaps the foreign-born disparity could be

Table 6.2.   Average Wealth of Adult Males in 1860 Standardized for
Age and Slave Values among those Living in the United
States and Standardized for Age among Those Living in
the North and Northeast

Country, state, or region of birth (but not necessarily of residence)	Average wealth in U.S. not standardized	Average wealth standardized for age living in the U.S.			
		If no slaves (1)	If average number of slaves (2)	Living in North (3)	Living in Northeast (4)
1. Me., N.H., Vt.	$2,580	$2,181	$2,675	$2,164	$1,968
2. Conn., Mass., R.I.	3,417	2,848	3,342	2,991	2,904
3. N.Y., N.J.	2,926	2,810	3,307	2,719	2,977
4. Pa.	2,348	2,082	2,576	2,221	2,437
5. Ohio	1,625	2,163	2,657	2,040	1,832
6. Ind., Ill., Mich.	1,192	1,899	2,393	1,884	—
7. Southern states	3,879	2,437	2,931	2,191	2,299
10. England, Scotland, Wales	1,822	1,501	1,995	1,467	1,933
12. Germany	1,247	990	1,484	1,266	1,314
13. Ireland	1,021	935	1,429	1,080	1,080

Source: Spin sample of 13,696 of 1860 (see n. 4).

Note: Dash indicates data not available.

attributed in part to religious differences or national policies
with respect to literacy and education. (I have found statistically significant results for various religious and literacy
groups in Ontario in 1871.[5]) Column (2) of table 6.2 is an
estimate based on the assumption that each nativity group
had the same proportion of men living in the South (.279)
and the average number of slaves. This in effect adds almost
$500 to the average for each group listed in column (1).
Results for column (3) were obtained by working only with
sample figures of men living in the North while those of
column (4) were obtained for those living only in the Northeast.[6] The fact flows from these latter two columns that
birth groups seemed to have about the same average wealth

no matter where they lived. We will need to make further
checks before confirming this hypothesis.

What are the time implications of the standardized averages in terms of the number of years that one birth group
leads another? Let us compare regions 2 and 3 with 4 and 5,
or roughly New York with Ohio. Using values of $2,800
and $2,200 and a growth rate of 1-2 percent per person, we
obtain a period of time between 24 and 12 years [2,800/
$2,200=(1.01)^{24} = (1.02)^{12}$]; the people of one region lag a
half generation or more behind those of the other region.
Use of a $1,900 value for region 6 leads to the possibility
of a generation gap between a native of New York and a
native of Illinois. Larger disparities exist between individuals in regions 10 and 13. That the Yankee average is approximately three times the Irish average implies a gap of
several generations. It would be revealing to know whether
or not the wealth average today of the descendants only of
the Irish of that period would be very much different in
real terms from the average of Yankees in 1860. We have
seen that the average for nonwhites today is significantly
less than that of whites a century ago.

Birth and Residence Areas

An interesting aspect of birth figures stems from further
classification by residence areas. Did Yankees who moved
to the Northwest do worse or better in the game of accumulation than their brothers who remained in the Northeast?
Some might argue that those who moved were the poorer
individuals who could not do well in the Northeast. This
line of reasoning would fall within the framework of the
safety valve theory. It would be within the bounds of Social
Darwinism since the fittest would remain in the East. Alter-
natively, it could be argued that those who were aggressive
moved with the frontier. They had the entrepreneurial
spirit to skim the capital gains of the earliest settlement.

There is a prevailing wisdom in much of the literature of
settlement that those who accumulated the most bought on
the frontier, sold it later, and moved to the farther frontier
in order to obtain the greatest percentage increase in price
per acre.[7] I hope the reader is not dissatisfied with the statistical results. They show that eastern birth was associated
with equal levels of wealth in the West and East; we see
these results in the small table.

Birth	*Residence area in 1860*					
area	NE			NW		
	TE	G_{TE}	age	TE	G_{TE}	age
NE	$2,704	.81	39.3	$2,669	.75	39.4

A regression equation fitted to this same population is TE =
$1,610 + $107 age + $189 nA - $38 NW$_{res}$. Surely the $38
coefficient associated with living in the Northwest rather
than the Northeast (after adjusting for age and occupation)
is of no practical consequence. The similarity in average
wealth, and even in average age, is phenomenal. Almost all
those born in the Northwest lived in the Northwest. Their
average wealth and age were $1,335 and 30.8. It is also of
interest to study those born in the North or South who
transferred to the other region. Might not northerners who
moved South be more aggressive? Might not southerners
who moved North be conscientious and frugal? The accompanying table shows that the statistical results again lead to
a draw.

Birth	*Residence area in 1860*					
area	North			South		
	TE	G_{TE}	age	TE	G_{TE}	age
North	$2,417	.80	37.6	$4,305	.85	36.9
South	2,484	.75	41.0	4,290	.84	37.4

It is tempting to infer that the foreign born of a country

who came to the United States also represented a proportional sample of the rich, middle, and poor groups of that country. The evidence can be determined only indirectly by a study of inequality. The figures needed have been given in table 6.1. There is an eye-catching similarity in the concentration coefficients for total estate. Connecticut, Massachusetts, and Rhode Island nativity gives a coefficient of .82. English, Scottish, and Welsh nativity gives one of .83. The German figure is .81. The only figure out of line is that for the Irish (.90). But can we be certain this was not the relative dispersion in that country? We do know that there were a few rich Irish in this country and only a few in Ireland. If all the emmigrants from a given country had been from a homogeneous group, be it poor or rich, its relative dispersion would be quite small. If only poor and rich had come, dispersion would have been larger. No real hints about differences in inequality among foreign born compared to native born are obtained from analysis of residence regions. (In the North, the equation for native born is $G_{TE} = .98 - .0048$ age $- .078$ NW_{res} and that for foreign born is $G_{TE} = 1.02 - .0049$ age $- .091$ NW_{res}.) Inequality among foreign born was only slightly greater than among native born. The poor from foreign lands were not relatively poorer than the rich from foreign lands.

There is a thesis that foreign born had to remain on the East Coast because they had no money. If this were true, one would expect that average wealth of foreign born would be greater in the Northwest than the Northeast for individuals of comparable age and nativity. Regression equations negate this assumption. For foreign born living in the North, $TE_{FB} = -\$458 + \$45$ age $- \$59$ NW_{res}, $\overline{TE}_{FB} = \$1,161$. This equation demonstrates that after adjustment for age, there was a 5 percent (59/1,161) differential disadvantage for those living in the Northwest, an indication that there was no advantage to living in the Northwest in 1860. It is true that there was a difference in the foreign-born mixture

in the two regions just as there was in the native-born mixture. Detailed stratification shows that English did better in
the Northeast than in the Northwest, whereas the reverse
was true for the Irish. Germans did equally well in the two
regions. These regional residence differences did not exist
or were not prominent among specific native-born groups.

It is unfortunate that one cannot be a little more specific
in stating a development model. It would be enticing to include a variable for birth area of parents and a variable for
number of years of residence in a given area. But area of
birth seems much more significant than area of *residence*
in the determination of an individual's wealth. An example
of evidence for this statement is the regression equation for
native-born men residing in the North in 1860:
$TE_{North\ res,\ NB} = -\$1,859 + \$104\ age + \$40\ NE_{res} +$
$\$422\ NE_{bir}$. The coefficient for birth is 10 times as large as
that for residence. Where you were born seemingly was
more important than where you lived, at least from the
standpoint of average total estate. This statement must be
limited either to persons living in the North or to whites
living in the South.[8]

Wealth in the 2,068 Counties

It is fascinating to compare wealth averages in the counties
of the United States in 1860 because of the significant differences that appeared in local areas throughout the country.
Some characteristics of low-wealth and high-wealth counties
are available from the censuses of agriculture and manufacturing. An interesting table was provided in the published 1860
census, which listed the aggregate value of the individual
declarations of total estate for each county. If each aggregate is divided by the number of adult freemen (af) in that
county, rough averages can be obtained. The TE values obtained will often be labeled ($0/af) or ($900/afs) to distinguish these estimates from those of the spin sample. The

former will signify aggregate wealth (including slave values in the South) divided by the number of adult free males. The latter will designate a subtraction of $900 for each slave in the county and a denominator of the number of adult-free and adult-slave males in the county. The ($0/af) values are given in table 6.3 for the 2,068 counties with complete data.[9]

Table 6.3. Average Wealth of Free Men in Each of 2,068 Counties in 1860 Classified by Slave Area

$X = TE = (\$0/af)$ Average wealth of county (lower class limit)	Number of counties			Assuming each man has average wealth of his county					
				Cumulative number of free men in the counties above X			A_X, cumulative wealth of the N_X free men		
	All	North	South	All	North	South	All	North	South
$ 0	266	211	55	1.000	1.000	1.000	1.000	1.000	1.000
1,000	704	478	226	.950	.940	.978	.988	.940	.996
2,000	460	230	230	.621	.544	.940	.794	.672	.918
3,000	170	44	126	.215	.092	.531	.436	.147	.781
4,000	116		116	.112		.397	.308		.676
5,000	254		254	.077		.274	.251		.551
10,000	63		63	.019		.066	.098		.216
15,000	23		23	.006		.022	.043		.213
20,000	12		12	.002		.005	.015		.029
	2,068	963	1,105						

	All	North	South
Number of freemen in millions	7.1	5.1	2.0
Mean total estate, $0/af	$2,700	$2,043	$4,380
Inequality coefficient G	.320	.186	.383

Sources: Mortality and Miscellaneous Statistics, 1860, table 3, pp. 296-319 for aggregate wealth in each county; *Census of Population, 1860*, pp. 2-592 for the number of white and free-colored men 20 and older (see also n. 10).

Note: Blank space indicates there were no frequencies in this range.

County Distributions

The frequency distributions of table 6.3 give detailed support to the findings that there was much greater area inequality in the South than in the North.[10] No county in the North had an average of more than $4,000, whereas 468 counties exceeded this level in the South. These 468 counties had only 11 percent of the freemen in the country but had 30 percent of its wealth. The coefficients of inequality of county wealth in the United States, the North, and the South were, respectively, .32, .19, and .38. Area inequality was twice as large in the South as in the North. It would be much more difficult to make generalizations about local conditions in the South in the antebellum period because of the varying wealth levels. A novel dealing with economic well-being in one county might not be at all typical of another. According to one interpretation of the Gini coefficient, if two counties are picked at random from the South, one would have wealth twice as large as that of the other.[11] It could be noted that the average wealth from the spin sample in the North was exactly the same as that of the ($0/af) average of the county table but that the spin-sample average for the South is 9 percent less than the ($0/af) figure of the South. It would be expected that the ($0/af) average would be higher because the wealth of women and children is included in the total.[12]

Economic Characteristics

Table 6.4 lists some characteristics of low-wealth counties which have the attributes of frontier counties since their population density is quite low and they were mostly in the Northwest. The adult population tended to be young, foreign born, and without families. The number of farms per adult and the improved acreage of farms were small. There were fewer people engaged in manufacturing (including lumbering) and wage rates were relatively high.

Table 6.4. Characteristics of the 963 Low-, Middle-, and High-Wealth
          Counties in the North in 1860

Characteristic	All	*$0-999*	*$1,000-1,999*	*$2,000-2,999*	*$3,000-3,999*
			Wealth classes		
1. Number of counties	963	209	479	231	44
2. Proportion of adult male population	1.00	.06	.40	.45	.09
3. Proportion of counties in class in Northwest	.78	.98	.81	.64	.41
4. Adult males in class as proportion of total population in class	.33	.45	.30	.29	.30
5. Average total estate ($0/af)	$1,610	606	1,521	2,377	3,324
6. Improved acreage as a proportion of improved plus un-improved acreage in class (I)	.45	.23	.44	.62	.68
7. Cash value per acre of improved or un-improved acreage in class (CV)	$27	$6	16	61	78
8. Number of farms per adult male	.29	.17	.34	.30	.26
9. Gini coefficient of inequality of acreage per farm	.32	.22	.34	.35	.39
10. Proportion of adult males in manufactur-ing in class (mfg)	.088	.079	.075	.116	.124
11. Annual wage rate	$279	231	287	299	310
12. Median age of adult males	34.0	32.2	34.1	35.0	35.1
13. Proportion of total population in class that is foreign born (FB)	17.0	27.0	14.6	13.5	13.7
14. Longitude in degrees	90	97	89	85	82
15. Latitude in degrees	41.5	42.1	41.4	41.3	40.6
16. Number of adult males per square mile (density D)	26.0	1.5	8.4	68.2	112.4

Sources: Population Census, 1860, including table 1 and pp. 527-32,
543, 544; *Mortality and Miscellaneous Statistics, 1860,* including
table 3 and pp. 166, 184, 219, 350, 493, 656 as examples from one area.

Note: Averages struck from county figures are unweighted. Denominators are the number of counties. Wages are the average annual cost of
labor per employee in manufacturing.

Chart 6.1. Average Wealth in 963 Northern Counties in the United States in 1860 Classified by Longitude

Wealth per adult
male ($0/af)

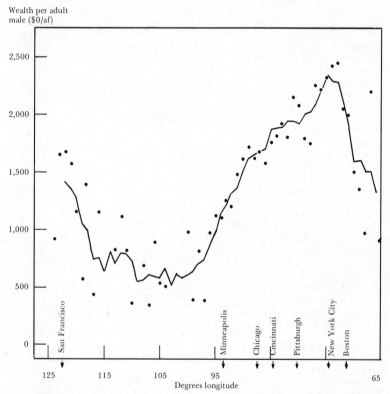

Sources: See table 6.4 and U.S. Department of Agriculture map of 1860, National Archives Record Group no. 83.

Note: An ($0/af) point for each degree of longitude and its unweighted, centered, 5° moving average.

Longitude: It is worthwhile to make an analysis in terms of longitude when studying the east-to-west movement. Chart 6.1 shows that wealth per adult male in the North was low in Maine and then rose to its peak in the longitudinal range from Boston to Philadelphia. It then decreased steadily to Omaha and remained low until it rose again in the Far West. The author traced counties intersected by the 41st parallel from New York to Nebraska and agricultural counties contiguous along the same general route and found the same pattern as that in chart 6.1. The drop from New York to Nebraska is about $1,700 in 1,400 miles, or a decrement of a little more than a dollar a mile.

There is one warning that must be given for the study of longitude. One should not allow distance to unduly influence his reasoning. The majority of the population west of Pennsylvania (our area labeled NW) is still east of Minneapolis in 1860. Only 11 percent of the population of adult males in nonslave states in 1860 were west of the Mississippi River. Wealth in the Northwest was substantial, actually 80 percent of that in the Northeast.

Table 6.5 allows us to inspect some characteristics of men for every 10° of longitude in moving from the East to the West Coast. Adult males form a larger portion of the population in the West, but they are younger. The median age of these people decreases about 5 years between the two coasts. If adult age begins at 20, in the West it was only two-thirds that in the East, and one might expect wealth averages to be only two-thirds as great because of this variable. Surprisingly, the proportion of foreign born among *all* persons of all ages was twice as large in the West as in the East. An individual was more likely to have been foreign born if he lived west of Pennsylvania. The statistical relationship among total estate, age, and nativity found from regression equations fitted to the 963 counties unweighted for population size compares favorably with our spin-sample results presented earlier in this chapter and in chapter 3.[13] This

Table 6.5. Characteristics of the 963 Western, Central, and Eastern Counties in the North in 1860

Characteristic	West	Longitudinal degrees					East
	129-120	119-110	109-100	99-90	89-80	79-70	69-60
1. Number of counties	72	30	12	283	361	195	10
2. Proportion of adult male population that is in the class	.04	.01	.01	.08	.33	.51	.02
3. Proportion of counties in the class that are in NW	1.0	1.0	1.0	1.0	.98	0	0
4. Adult males in class as proportion of total	.52	.40	.29	.30	.25	.26	.25
5. Average total estate ($0/af) = TE	$1,572	831	723	1,172	1,763	2,161	1,325
6. Improved acreage as proportion of improved plus unimproved acreage in class (I)	.34	.56	.25	.26	.51	.64	.45
7. Cash value per acre (CV)	$9.	6.	5.	9.	22.	77.	13.
8. Number of farms per adult male	.15	.02	.01	.28	.36	.27	.35
9. Gini coefficient of inequality of acreage per farm	.36	.14	.33	.28	.35	.36	.33

10. Proportion of adult males in manufacturing in class (mfg)	.08	.05	.02	.04	.08	.18	.14
11. Annual wage rate	$569	380	257	211	275	265	217
12. Median age of adult males	31.7	32.6	32.0	32.4	34.2	36.7	36.7
13. Proportion of total population in class that is foreign born (FB)	.26	.30	.12	.19	.15	.13	.07
14. Longitude in degrees	122	115	105	94	86	75	69
15. Latitude in degrees	42.1	39.1	36.8	42.2	40.9	41.8	44.7
16. Number of adult males per square mile (density D)	11.2	.7	.3	2.6	9.4	102.3[a]	10.7
17. Average real estate	$819	339	249	815	1,312	1,477	822
18. Average personal estate	$753	491	473	356	450	683	503

Sources: See table 6.4 and chart 6.1.

Note: Averages struck from county figures are unweighted. Denominators are the number of counties. The intersections are roughly 70 in western Maine, 80 in very western Pennsylvania, 90 at the eastern tip of Iowa, 100 in mid-Nebraska, 110 in eastern Utah, and 120 in mid-Oregon.

[a]New York County is one of the counties.

agreement adds confidence to expressions we can now
develop with some new variables.

Improved Acreage: All the indexes of table 6.5 generally
reflect downward movement in going from east to west.
The improvement index (I), the proportion of improved
plus unimproved acreage that was cleared or improved,
reveals the huge task of clearing farmland that faced
western settlers. This accomplishment was reflected in
part in the cash value of land and the value of total estate,
which we can see in the accompanying table. Wealth in-

100I	n(counties)	TE	100I	n(counties)	TE
00-09	71	$ 830	50-59	119	$1,848
10-19	104	1,013	60-69	150	2,165
20-29	124	1,157	70-79	95	2,361
30-39	107	1,323	80-89	39	2,237
40-49	133	1,580	90-99	21	1,658
				963	

creases somewhat linearly when classified by our improvement index. A regression equation, TE = $730 + $1,970 I,
n = 963, indicates that total estate would be $730 if there
were no improved acreage and $2,700 if it were fully im-
proved. Suppose it took a generation to clear the land. The
implication for growth of 2,700/730 in a 25-30-year
period is a rate of 4.5-5.5 percent a year. Perhaps it is not
coincidence that this range is not much different from
that suggested in chapter 3 as the average annual growth
rate of accumulation for individuals. The distribution of
farmland among farm *owners* was quite constant across
the country but the number of farms per person was lower
in the West. There was one peculiar exception. The number of farms per person in the 10° from Iowa to Nebraska
was as high as that in the 10° from Maine to Ohio. Manufacturing also absorbed many more persons in the East
than in the West. One exception to the various patterns
was wages in manufacturing, which was greater in the

West and relatively constant among other longitudinal classes.

Density: The relationship between total estate and density, or persons per square mile, was strong. This stems from the fact that real estate values are obviously dependent in part on population pressures and the length of time or history needed to bring settlement of large masses of people. The accompanying table shows the relationship between density and average wealth.

D = density, number of adult males (afs) per square mile	n(counties)		Average wealth		
			TE_{North}	TE_{South}	
	North	South	($0/af)	($0/af)	($900/afs)
0.0- .99	237	130	$ 987	$2,356	$1,284
1.0- 1.99	65	132	1,181	3,310	1,498
2.0- 4.99	124	396	1,402	4,029	1,430
5.0- 9.99	241	349	1,663	6,510	1,680
10.0- 19.99	212	78	2,154	5,925	2,201
20.0- 49.99	65	12	2,465	4,341	2,678
50.0- 99.99	9	4	2,560	4,679	2,539
100.0-9,999.99	10	4	2,476	2,480	2,283
	963	1,105			

One plausible depiction of the relationship between average total estate and density for the 963 northern counties is TE = $1000 D$^{.238}$; this equation for the year 1860 contains implications of wealth growth over time. The population of adult males increased about 4 percent a year from 1850 to 1860; therefore we might substitute $D = 1.04^t$ in the above equation, where t is time. When this is done, there is an implication that average total estate grows 1 percent each year. I have shown in chapter 3 that per capita growth of wealth has been 1-2 percent a year. It is remarkable that this factor appeared in attenuated form as a population density factor in 1860. A ramification of the 1860 equations is that a county with a density of 1-2 persons per square mile was between 76 and 38 years in time behind a county of average density (26 persons per square mile). Thus a frontier county was roughly two generations behind a county of average wealth.[14]

Population density or time can be a proxy for changes in many variables. The elasticity coefficient for density derived from statistical data is smaller when other variables are explicitly introduced into the equations. An obvious example of an important variable determining cash value of land per acre in a county (CV) is the proportion of this land that has been cleared or improved (I). A very high correlation coefficient is obtained when CV is related to I and population density D for the 963 northern counties. In this case the elasticity coefficient of cash value is .51 with respect to improvement and .28 with respect to density. The extent of improvement, albeit a farmland measure, is more significant than density in the statistical sense. Cash value of land in a county is fairly closely related to average total estate in a county.[15]

The analysis of the elasticities of different variables can become rather complex since cash value of land is only one ingredient in the determination of wealth in a county. Obviously the level of wages, or better, the proportion of men in the county engaged in manufacturing is a vital determinant of average total estate in that county. Significant correlations are obtained when total estate is related to cash value and wage rates or to improved acreage and the proportion of men in manufacturing.[16] These equations do indicate that the agricultural sector or the real estate sector was more important than the manufacturing sector in determining the wealth of individuals in 1860.

Counties bordering the Mississippi River

The location and statistics for the rich areas among America's 2,000 or more counties are enticing. Of the 12 counties in the United States averaging more than $20,000

in total estate ($0/af) in 1860, 5 were in Mississippi, 4 in
Louisiana, 2 in Alabama, and 1 in South Carolina. Seven
were cotton and sugar counties bordering the Mississippi
River, which represented a significant portion of total
wealth. Let us list the counties in 1860 bordering the Mississippi River from Memphis to its outlet, noting the average wealth (see table 6.6). Tensas County, Louisiana, had
the highest freeman average in the country. Of its 552
adult males, 111 had 50 or more slaves. The second- and
third-highest freeman averages in the United States were
Isaquena and Wilkinson counties in Mississippi. The wealth
average ($0/af) of the 36 border counties was 5.2 times that
in the United States.

We can make an adjustment for slave wealth by subtracting $900 times the number of slaves from aggregate wealth
in the county. If the subtracted amount is greater than
aggregate personal estate, aggregate real estate is used. The
net aggregate may be divided by the number of adult free
men ($900/af) or by the number of adult free and slave
males ($900/afs). Each of these ratios is an average of non-
human wealth; the latter is the adaption of the postwar
condition. Whereas our 36 border counties had a $0/af
average 5.2 times that in the United States, they had a
$900/afs average, which was only 80 percent of the $900/afs
average in the United States. This was an economy whose
wealth values consisted largely of slaves. The extreme case
in the table was the county across the river from Natchez
(Concordia), with an average of 30 slaves per adult white.
Orleans County (New Orleans) actually had fewer slaves per
white male adult than the United States had as a whole.

Counties with High Nonhuman Wealth

The distribution of county wealth in the United States
for four possible concepts is given in table 6.7. There is
merit in the second situation, $900/af, because hypothetically

Table 6.6. Wealth of Counties bordering the Mississippi River in 1860 (from Memphis to New Orleans)

West side of the river

$0/af ($900/afs) s/af			County name
Arkansas			
$5,330	($1,840)	2	Crittendon
10,300	(2,510)	5	Phillips
10,490	(2,860)	4	Arkansas
11,850	(3,530)	4	Desha
11,410	(1,150)	1	Chicot
Louisiana			
19,840	(2,650)	10	Carroll
26,100	(1,290)	19	Madison
53,000	(3,210)	26	Tensas
16,700	(100)	30	Concordia
14,290	(1,480)	9	Pointe Coupee
13,730	(1,550)	15	Feliciana W.
18,830	(2,190)	10	Baton Rouge W.
18,330	(1,970)	10	Iberville
8,400	(1,610)	4	Assumption
5,870	(1,360)	3	Lafourche
20,870	(1,300)	13	St. Charles
4,470	(1,520)	1	Jefferson
8,570	(1,420)	5	Palquemines

East side of the river

County name	$0/af ($900/afs) s/af		
Tennessee			
Shelby (Memphis)	$7,290	($4,400)	1
Mississippi			
De Sota	10,090	(2,140)	5
Tunica	10,950	(1,340)	11
Coahoma	18,890	(2,670)	10
Bolivar	17,110	(1,350)	17
Washington			
Isaquena	26,800	(1,130)	32
Warren	13,740	(2,630)	6
Claiborne	21,600	(2,410)	13
Jefferson	22,740	(2,150)	14
Adams (Natchez)	14,910	(2,130)	8
Wilkinson	26,100	(1,510)	19
Louisiana			
Feliciana E.	13,730	(1,550)	9
Baton Rouge E.	6,370	(1,370)	3
Ascension	13,560	(1,900)	7
St. James	11,710	(1,180)	9
St. John the Baptist	8,340	(1,250)	5
Orleans (New Orleans)	2,170	(1,770)	.3
St. Bernard	5,250	(960)	3

Source: See table 6.3. These are not spin-sample data.

Note: The unweighted arithmetic mean of the 36 counties was 13,940 (1,772) 10. The mean for all persons in the United States regardless of county was 2,700 (1,973) .56. It is to be remembered that the average real estate value (or average personal estate value in 16 Louisiana parishes)

Table 6.6 *(cont.)*

is substituted for the $900/afs if it is larger than the $900/afs. The
average wealth of freemen is $0/af; in parentheses the average wealth
of all men after deducting the value of slaves at $900 each is
($900/afs); and the average number of slaves per freemen is s/af.

Table 6.7. Means and Inequality of Each of 2,068 Counties in 1860
under Four Possible Conditions of Slavery

X Average wealth of county (lower class limit)	*($0/af)*		*($900/af)*		*($0/afs)*		*($900/afs)*	
	Number of counties	N_X	*Number of counties*	N_X	*Number of counties*	N_X	*Number of counties*	N_X
$ 0	266	1.000	335	1.000	269	1.000	454	1.000
1,000	704	.950	919	.939	791	.955	1,075	.913
2,000	460	.621	487	.556	559	.639	442	.484
3,000	170	.215	177	.147	309	.235	85	.089
4,000	116	.112	53	.036	90	.068	10	.006
5,000	352	.077	97	.023	50	.028	2	.001
	2,068		2,068		2,068		2,068	

(Number of af or afs men in thousands)

	7,066	7,066	7,928	7,928

(Arithmetic mean wealth)

	$2,700	$2,213	$2,407	$1,973

(Gini coefficient G)

	.320	.235	.230	.209

Note: $0/af = wealth value, including value of slaves, per white and
free colored adult male. $900/af = wealth value, not including value
of slaves (assuming each was worth $900) per white and free colored
adult male. $0/afs = wealth value, including value of slaves, per adult
(white, free colored, and slave adult) male. $900/afs = wealth value,
net of slaves at $900 each, per adult male. N_X is the cumulative num-
ber of men in the counties above X, assuming each man has the average wealth of his county.

there are only freemen in the numerator and denominator of the average. The results give some notion of what might have been the distribution of nonhuman wealth among the free. Note for the averages that ($900/af)/($0/af) is $2,213/$2,700 = .82. We thus take away 18 percent of aggregate wealth of the rich counties and expect less area inequality. The Gini coefficient in the latter cases is computed to be 73 percent of that in the former case. This is a calculation of how much area inequality would have dropped had there been no slaves.

The fourth distribution of table 6.7 is that of $900/afs for counties in the United States. Here one has a hypothetical approximation of a postbellum census: individuals of all colors would declare their nonhuman wealth. The average of $1,973 is the value one might use for comparison with the average wealth from the 1870 census.[17] The subtraction of slave wealth and the addition of slaves as zero wealthholders decrease area inequality from .32 to .21. Area inequality for southern counties decreases from .38 to .24 in adjusting for slavery. This level is significantly lower but it remains higher than the area inequality coefficient in the North. The slave economy was largely responsible for greater area inequality in the South.

The counties with the highest $900/af averages form an array still dominated by those in the delta area. The top 25 counties, those with an average above $8,000, include 10 counties in Louisiana and 9 in Mississippi. Rich slaveholders held substantial wealth in real estate as well as in slaves. The postbellum approximation, $900/afs, gives new county leaders. The county with the greatest wealth in this list of 2,068 is Davidson County, Tennessee, which includes Nashville and the Hermitage, the home of Andrew Jackson. The next two counties have very few individuals and are located in Texas; they are followed by Bourbon County, Kentucky. Shelby County (Memphis) is ninth. One must treat these ranks as only general indications. It is possible that in smaller counties men may have had wealth in slaves in other counties so that the subtraction process does not adequately eliminate all slaveholdings. The listing shows a belt of rich counties running north and south of Nashville that includes the 14th (Maury County, the home of James Polk) and two other counties ranked 21st and 33rd in the array.

The northern county with greatest wealth, Bergen County, New Jersey, was 12th with an average of $3,994. The 13th was Ramsey County (St. Paul), Minnesota. Queens, Westchester, and Richmond counties, New York, were 25, 30, and 36. Many very small counties, led by eight counties in Texas, had large wealth. Second on the list was Refugie County, Texas, with an average wealth of $4,828. It had only 378 adult males, including 40 adult male slaves. Delta counties, of course, are far down the list. Suppose a county had 30 slaves per free man or 8 adult slaves per free man. Increasing the denominator of the mean to 9 times its former size has a great effect in adjusting for slavery. The majority of the 36 counties in table 6.6 are in the bottom half of the 2,068 on our new list. Slavery was vital to southern rich. Charleston County, South Carolina (Charleston), had an average of $7,292 on the ($0/af) list and $1,688 on the ($900/afs) list. The majority of counties at the bottom of the postbellum array had sparse populations. A few of the counties with large population at the bottom were in Maine and, surprisingly, in California.

Summary

We have made a detailed analysis for 1860 of average wealth of men classified by area of birth. The areas of birth included Ireland $1,000; Germany $1,200; Holland, Switzerland, and Scandinavia $1,400; England, Scotland, and Wales $1,800; northern native born $2,400; southern native born $4,200; and all nonslaves $2,600. Among native born there

is a clear gradient. The figures are Connecticut, Massachusetts, and Rhode Island $3,400; New York and New
Jersey $2,900; Pennsylvania $2,300; Ohio $1,600; and
Indiana, Illinois, and Michigan $1,200. This native-born
gradient is not so severe after adjustment for age, but it is
still very much in evidence. An unsupported hypothesis is
that those born in the East were more likely to represent
second- or third-generation Americans who had been
accumulating wealth for a long period.

Division of northern states at the Pennsylvania–Ohio
border gives what is called the NW and the NE. Some very
absorbing figures show that those born in the NE who lived
in the NW had almost the same mean as those born in the
NE living in the NE. Those who moved west with the frontier were neither more nor less dynamic in the game of
accumulation than those remaining in the NE. Yet those
born in the NW living in the NW did not fare so well (before and after adjustment for age). I can explain this result
only with the unsupported hypothesis that eastern ancestral
nativity provided inheritance of human and nonhuman
wealth.

An analysis is made of the wealth averages for 1860 freemen of 963 northern counties and 1,105 southern counties.
The counties of low wealth are most often frontier counties
in the NW of low population density, composed of young
men without families with a greater than average probability
of being foreign born. The number of farms per adult and
the improved acreage of farms were small. Low-wealth
counties had few engaged in manufacturing but had relatively high wages.

Surprising to some would be the fact that counties of high
density (adult males per square mile) had higher than average wealth in 1860. A county with 4 percent greater density
than another had about 1 percent more in mean wealth.
This finding implies that average wealth was growing about
1 percent a year because the population and density were

growing almost 4 percent. It is rather remarkable that
economic growth appeared in attenuated form as a population density factor in 1860. Similar time implications were
found in the case of the cash value of land and the proportion of land that was cleared or improved for the various
counties.

Area inequality for 1860 free men was extreme. If one
arrays the total estate values of the 2,068 counties and
weights each by its population, the resulting Lorenz curve
has an inequality coefficient G of .32. It was .38 for the
southern counties and .19 for northern counties. The South
was certainly not composed of counties with similar wealth
conditions. The extremely wealthy counties for 1860 free,
such as those bordering the Mississippi River from Memphis
to New Orleans, did become those below average in the
freedom of 1870.

7. The Significant Wealth Patterns

We have now concluded our study of the wealthholdings of adult males in the United States in the middle of the nineteenth century. Let us list in succinct form our major findings.

1. Was the United States a land of propertyholders? The answer, based on the evidence presented in the censuses, is that there were probably fewer who had wealth than one might have expected. Of every five adult males, only about two reported having real estate, and about three reported having total estate. Although it is true that, among older groups, three of every five Americans had wealth in the form of real estate and four of every five had resources in the total estate category, it is also true that the remaining 20-40 percent were unable to accumulate wealth throughout their entire life spans.

These reported results were found to be consistent for each of the three census years. More technically, consider the proportions of adult males who were propertyholders (PH), personal estate holders (PEH), and total estate holder (TEH) defined, in turn, as the proportion having $1 or mor of real estate, the proportion having $100 or more of personal estate, and the proportion having $100 or more of total estate. We studied these proportions for nonslaves in 1850 and 1860, for whites only in 1870, and for whites and nonwhites combined in 1870. The accompanying table lists the proportions. These simple measurements help to

	1850	1860	1870 white	1870 all
PH	.41	.43	.43	.39
PEH	—	.58	.57	.53
TEH	—	.62	.62	.57

summarize several points. There was little or no change in wealth participation rates from 1850 to 1860 and from

1860 to 1870 for whites. Differences between 1870 white and 1870 all are explained by the fact that the latter contained 11 percent nonwhites. The 1860 and 1870 figures are the first of many indications that the Civil War did little to change the distribution of nonhuman wealth among whites. In all cases the proportions of ownership for the three points in time are shockingly low. It is quite evident that every adult male in the United States did not own property. Actually, in 1850 fewer than half owned any land in a country where frontier land was being sold at $1.25 per acre. The have-nots constituted a strong proportion of adult males in the middle of the nineteenth century. In spite of changes in certain American institutions, this proportion remained constant from decade to decade.

2. Accumulation of real estate depended, in part, on inheritance, knowledge of markets and credit, facility in reading and writing English or at least some foreign language, physical health, desire to accumulate, and many other factors, including luck. It is not surprising that the probability of owning real estate varied for occupational and nativity groups. Surely the probability of ownership would be higher for farmers than for nonfarmers. One would also expect that the foreign born would be less likely to own real estate, not only because they were concentrated more in urban areas, but also because they were less likely to be familiar with American economic institutions.

Classifications of free men in 1850 demonstrate that the propertyholder proportion was twice as high for farmers as for nonfarmers, twice as high for native born as for foreign born, and twice as high for the old as for the young. A male who was young, foreign born, and a nonfarmer had the smallest probability of being a propertyholder. An older native-born farmer had a probability many times as great. Urban areas were the focal point for the native-born/foreign-born disparity. In such areas the old foreign born had the same probability of achievement as the young native born; one has the impression that the foreign-born father reached later life with no greater probability of ownership than that of his much younger son born in the United States.

The PH relationships of 1850 generally held for 1860 and 1870 white, although there was some degree of improvement among the foreign born. Differences in TEH among groups were not nearly so pronounced, at least in percentage terms. This is true because we are considering wealth in a wider context than land and buildings. Among all adult males for 1870, TEH was .66 for farmers and .48 for non-farmers, .59 for native born and .52 for foreign born. Thus the penalty, in terms of wealth participation, for being an urban dweller or foreign born was not severe by 1870.

3. Records of achievement in a given census year assume greater meaning when the men are classified by age group. Age conveys a record of time, of the history of the life cycles of individuals. The fact that older people were more likely to be property owners means that individuals, on the average, improved their economic conditions through time. Overall, the possibility of accomplishment existed even though, for the individual, the chance of obtaining wealth in any given year was small.

The probability of ownership increased with age, rising rapidly in younger adult years and reaching a maximum of about .80 at age 60. This parabola was an index of the improved chances of an individual's rising above at least a minimum standard of ownership as he progressed through his life cycle. The implication of the shapes of the parabolas is that the general level of PH or TEH did not change over time as people became older and new populations entered the labor force. Data on farm and home ownership from 1880 to 1930 or 1940 substantiate this finding.

How could this happen in the face of the rural-urban movement that presumably severed the ties people had with farmland and perhaps real estate? There is a decrease in the

depressing effect of foreign born, for the simple reason that
there were proportionally fewer in the population as a whole,
and a positive effect due to the fact that the average age of
adults was substantially higher in the 1960s than a century
earlier. In an experiment applied to the 1870 all values of
TEH for various age–nativity–occupation groups, the use of
population weights of 1960 revealed that the effect of increased age and decreased immigration was sufficient to
leave overall TEH in 1960 the same as it was in 1870. Actual
TEH in 1960 may have been slightly larger than for 1870
all, perhaps .68 instead of .62.

The reader may argue that shifts in average age and nativity
should not be considered real phenomena in the game of
capitalism. But they are as positively associated with frontier
settlement of available land as is the occupation of farming.
One is likely to forget the effect of age in discussing the
urban movement, not realizing that the proportion of foreign born among adult males reached its peak in 1860 and
1870, not later. Youth and foreign birth augmented the
probability of being a have-not in the agrarian era even as
manufacturing augmented the probability in later periods.

4. If America in the middle of the nineteenth century was
a country of western settlement, of the movement of men
from the East Coast, the expectation would be that conditions for wealth accumulation should be positively correlated to degrees of longitude. Certainly the propertyholder proportion in 1850 confirms this assumption, since
those living in the Northwest (west of the Ohio–Pennsylvania border) had a PH of .48 while those living in the Northeast had a PH of .36. However, the geographical factor is
somewhat difficult to isolate from other factors. We
studied PH and TEH by region of residence and place of
birth. In cross classifications and standardization those in
the Northwest did fare better, particularly in terms of owning real estate. In addition those in the Northwest who were
born in the Northeast had the highest estate-participation

rates. Perhaps Northeast birth was an index of higher probability of having native-born parents, of inheriting cultural as well as nonhuman wealth. Some interesting sidelights were that those born in England, Scotland, and Wales were more likely to be haves than those born in Germany and that the latter, in turn, were more likely to be haves than those born in Ireland.

5. We turn now to the dollar amounts of wealth owned by individuals in the three census years of our investigation. The general conclusion in studying average wealth is that free men in the United States at midcentury did very well indeed. Measures of relative dispersion or inequality, however, have some rather disconcerting aspects for a country generally characterized as egalitarian in nature.

The arithmetic mean of real estate held by adult nonslave males in 1850 was $\overline{RE}$ = \$1,001, a most magnificent amount (about \$4,000 in 1970 prices). However, there was extreme scatter from this average. A general measure of relative inequality is the Gini coefficient of concentration, G, which varies between 1.0 if one man held all wealth and 0.0 if each man had the same wealth; for 1850 this measure was G = .857, an index of very large inequality. A concise form of the distribution in 1850 appears in the informal table.

Real estate (lower class limit)	Percentage of men	Percentage of aggregate real estate
0	59.0	0.
1	1.0	—
100	18.0	8.
1,000	21.0	54.
10,000	1.7	32.
100,000	.03	6.
	100.0	100.

This is our first glimpse of the rich in this country at this early date. Only 22 percent of men were above the mean while 78 percent were below. The top 1.0 percent held 30 percent of all real estate. Inequality of propertyholding was substantially larger than most people might have guessed. It could even be characterized as extreme.

We found similar results for other years for real estate (RE), personal estate (PE), and total estate (TE). A further example is that of total estate for 1870 all, where the average wealth was $\overline{TE}$ = \$2,399 and inequality of wealth was G = .833. The accompanying table provides a succinct distribution. Again, 22 percent are above the mean. The

Total estate (lower class limit)	Percentage of men	Percentage of aggregate total estate
0	43.0	0.
1	1.0	—
100	23.0	4.
1,000	28.0	40.
10,000	5.3	47.
100,000	.15	9.
	100.0	100.

top 1.0 percent held 26 percent of wealth; the top 2.0 percent held 37 percent. The logarithms of the positive RE and positive TE values form excellent normal curves with relative standard deviations similar to that for I.Q.s. The wealth of an individual is determined by age, nativity, occupation, residence, inheritance of both nonhuman and human (or cultural) gifts, education, physical fitness, ability, drive, and luck. (Illiterate men, for example, had mean wealth only one-fifth as large as that held by all men.) How could these factors have combined in such a way as to produce the maldistribution that actually existed? How could the myth of self-betterment have been accepted so readily?

6. The answer to these questions must be that self-betterment does pervade the jungle of inequality. It is most poignantly revealed in age classifications where older groups possess more than younger groups. A large part of this book is devoted to the study of wealth and age in a given year because quantifications represent betterment for the average

individual. These quantifications also give us clues to per capita growth over time for the country as a whole.

We found that individuals experienced two types of growth during their life cycles as their wealth increased about 6 percent a year on the average: (1) a general improvement rate of 1.0-2.0 percent a year arising over time from economic growth of wealth per person and (2) an apparent growth rate of about 4.5-5.0 percent a year arising from aging. The estate–age pattern of the population in a given year was slightly parabolic but was essentially a straight line from age 20 to 69. The line could be specified as TE = b(adult age) or, for 1870 total estate, as TE = $112(age - 18)$. This line rotated or shifted upward each year as the slope b increased about 1.5 percent. In any year the slope amounted to 4.5-5.0 percent of average wealth. There is an implication that the degree of rotation (.015) is consistent with apparent growth minus population growth at the time (.045 - .030). Thus, the average individual experienced handsome gains in real wealth as he progressed through life. This differential must have been observable and easily apparent in spite of the very wide scatter, or inequality, from the average wealth for a specific year of age. This gain even occurred from 1860 to 1870, when there was an absence of general economic growth.

7. There is no question that a sizable portion of total wealth was held by a small proportion of the people in each census year studied. For example, the top 2 percent of men generally held somewhere between 35 and 45 percent of wealth, and the top 5 percent most often held 50-60 percent for most of the main subsets of the population. These shares may have been small compared to those held by individuals in England and other European countries but they were nevertheless significant. There very definitely was an elite upper group in America in terms of control of economic resources.

We can see further ramifications of inequality from the

Gini coefficients for the various types of wealth in the accompanying table. Thus, there was a revealing constancy

	1850	*1860*	*1870 white*	*1870 all*
G_{RE}	.86	.85	.84	.86
G_{PE}	—	.87	.84	.85
G_{TE}	—	.83	.81	.83

in inequality from 1850 to 1870. Note that this is true for the distribution of personal estate as well as for the distribution of real and total estate. Real estate value of farmers was substantially more unequal in distribution than was farmland acreage. This occurred in part because there were many who were landless and some who owned several large and fertile farms. Farmland inequality changed little from 1860 to 1930. There was an essential similarity in the South in 1860 of inequality of personal estate and inequality of slaveholdings. The same inequality of slaveholding existed in 1790.

8. The most important aspect of the entire study pertains to the change in wealthholding between 1860 and 1870. Did the disruption of the Civil War fundamentally alter the inequality of wealthholding of the free population? The response to this question, employing wealth statistics, must be complex since it must do more than show slaves who became free; it should indicate the changing holdings among the white population as well. It must also analyze the relative situations in the North and in the South. We quantify this analysis in the accompanying table. The $1,900 advan-

	$\overline{TE}$			G_{TE}		
	1860	*1870 white*	*1870 all*	*1860*	*1870 white*	*1870 all*
United States	$2,580	$2,691	$2,399	.832	.814	.833
North	2,040	2,921	2,884	.813	.810	.816
South	3,978	2,034	1,428	.845	.818	.866

tage in the South in 1860 was due almost entirely to the

fact that there were 2.0 slaves per adult white male in that region. A separate county analysis for the South in 1860 establishes the essential validity of an average value of $900 per slave. It is not surprising that freemen in 1860 in the South went from a twice to one-half position relative to those in the North in the decade from 1860 to 1870.

Wealth inequality among freemen in 1870 was the same as among freemen in 1860. The simplest explanation for this phenomenon is that inequality in the North remained constant while that in the South increased. The southern increase was due to the addition of former slaves to the set of freemen. The addition of these individuals at zero or near-zero wealth would have increased inequality even more had it not been for the lessened inequality brought about by the destruction of the wealthholdings of the very rich slaveholders. The United States coefficient was closer to that of the North in 1870 than in 1860 because, relatively, there was so much more wealth in the North in the later year. One must be very careful to note that, within the context of all human beings, the inequality drop from 1860 to 1870 was incalculable. Freedom is without price—it cannot be stated in terms of dollar values.

Some estimates of average *nonhuman* wealth of all adult males were made for 1850 and 1860. One could compare these estimates, net of the effect of slavery, directly with the 1870 all figures. The price-adjusted figures of the accompanying table show these comparative annual growth rates per adult male. Perhaps southern wealth in 1870

	1850 all–1860 all	*1860 all–1870 all*	*1850 all–1870 all*
United States	3.1%	− 0.9%	1.1%
North	2.3	0.0	1.2
South	4.9	− 4.0	0.3

resembled that in 1850. The rates in the United States and in the North are similar to those of estimates for income in this period. Let us not forget that our TE–age patterns indicate that the individual was accumulating 4.5-5.0 percent even though there might have been no general improvement.

9. A disheartening finding was that 1962 levels of non-whites were still below those of whites in 1870 after adjustment is made for price changes. However, the nonwhite distribution in 1870 had the incipient inequality of the white distribution in the same year.

10. The results of our studies of residence groups and nativity groups with respect to real estate and total estate only strengthened the general findings given in point 4 for holders of property and total estate. One interesting aspect of 1860 data for the North was that those born in the north-eastern part of the country who lived in the Northwest (Ohio and west) had the same $\overline{TE}$ as that of individuals born in the Northeast who remained in the Northeast.

11. Multiple regression equations developed for inequality of wealthholding in a given year showed that the Gini coefficient would be less if a population were older, substantially more if it were urban instead of rural, and that nativity had little to do with inequality, at least by 1870. Using these equations for a 1960 projection, we found that the reduced inequality attributable to aging counterbalanced a large part of the inequality that can be ascribed to the movement toward urban living. A Federal Reserve estimate for inequality in 1962-63 was about 5 percent less than that of the Gini coefficient in 1870, after adjustment for definitional differences.

12. There are three general findings from all the facets of this research on wealth in the United States. First of all, there was remarkable stability in the pattern of relative distribution of wealth among freemen in 1850, 1860, and 1870. Second, this inequality was surprisingly great; on the one hand, a few had large amounts of wealth, counter-balanced by the many who were essentially propertyless. Third, this inequality was tolerated because for the average person handsome rates of accumulation of wealth during his lifetime were within the realm of possibility.

Appendix Tables

Appendix table A1. Characteristics of Adult Males 20 and Older in the United States in 1860 Classified by Three Residence Regions and Four Birth Regions

Region of birth	Region of residence							
	Northeast		Northwest		South		All	
	Proportion holding real and total estate							
	PH	TEH	PH	TEH	PH	TEH	PH	TEH
Northeast	.44	.62	.57	.73	.43	.68	.47	.65
Northwest	.33	.53	.41	.58	.43	.63	.41	.58
South	.46	.68	.56	.72	.47	.69	.48	.69
Foreign born	.25	.45	.43	.58	.27	.49	.32	.50
All	.38	.57	.45	.64	.44	.66	.43	.62

Proportion who are farmers, average age, and number as a proportion of male population

Region of birth	$\bar{A}$	Age	N	$\bar{A}$	Age	N	$\bar{A}$	Age	N	$\bar{A}$	Age	N
Northeast	.45	39	.253	.58	39	.095	.37	39	.019	.48	39	.367
Northwest	.40	36	.002	.64	31	.089	.52	32	.007	.63	31	.098
South	.32	42	.013	.66	41	.050	.64	37	.213	.63	38	.276
Foreign born	.22	37	.116	.45	36	.103	.24	36	.039	.32	37	.258
All	.38	39	.384	.57	37	.338	.56	37	.279	.49	38	1.000

Source: The spin sample of 13,696 from schedule 1 of the 1860 census.

Note: The number born in the Northwest living outside the Northwest was small; standard errors for PH and TEH are as large as .01.

Appendix table A2. Proportion of Adult Males Holding Total Estate
Adjusted for Age and Occupational Differences
(TEH adjusted), Classified by Region of Birth
and Residence of Men in the United States in
1860

Region of birth	*Region of residence*		
	Northeast	*Northwest*	*South*
Northeast	.63	.70	.68
Northwest	.58	.65	.63
South	.61	.68	.67
Foreign born	.50	.57	.55

Note: Values are obtained from a regression equation fitted to the
spin-sample data of the form TEH = .1651 + .4765 log(age − 18) −
.1362 nA − .0800 NE_{res} − .0154 So_{res} + .0477 NE_{bir} + .0360 So_{bir}
− .0826 FB, R^2 = .19, N = 13,696. Each of the three birth and two
residence variables is a simple dichotomy with a value of 1 if an
individual has the attribute and 0 if he does not.

Appendix table A3. Number of Men with Personal Estate Less Than
$100 (1 − PEH) in the United States in 1860 and
1870 by Age, Nativity, and Occupation as a
Proportion of Male Population in Each Class

	Age			
	20 and up	*20-29*	*30-39*	*40-99*
	1 − PEH for 1860 nonslaves			
All men	.424	.63	.37	.27
Native born	.379	.60	.31	.22
Foreign born	.553	.72	.50	.44
Farmers	.318	.55	.26	.17
Nonfarmers	.528	.69	.46	.40
	1 − PEH for all in 1870			
All men	.473	.68	.40	.34
Native born	.449	.66	.37	.30
Foreign born	.545	.76	.49	.45
Farmers	.373	.61	.31	.24
Nonfarmers	.566	.75	.48	.45

Source: Spin samples of 13,696 and 9,823 from schedules 1 of 1860
and 1870 censuses, respectively.

Appendix table A4. Cumulative Proportion of Adult Men (N_{RE}) by
Real Estate Class in the United States, 1850-70

Lower class limit of estate class, RE	N_{RE}, *or proportion of men above class limit*			
	1850 free	*1860 free*	*1870 whites*	*1870 all*
$100,000	.00034	.00049	.00069	.00051
50,000	.0012	.0022	.0026	.0023
20,000	.0055	.011	.014	.013
10,000	.017	.031	.042	.037
5,000	.043	.076	.104	.092
2,000	.129	.184	.222	.198
1,000	.223	.281	.305	.272
500	.311	.359	.372	.333
200	.389	.414	.420	.378
100	.407	.427	.431	.389
50	.412	.430	.432	.391
1	.413	.431	.433	.391
0	1.00	1.00	1.00	1.00

Sources: Spin samples of 10,393, 13,696, and 9,823 from schedules
1 of the 1850-70 censuses. Populations of adult males in millions
were 5.01, 7.09, 8.69, and 9.83, respectively, for 1850 free, 1860
free, 1870 whites, and 1870 all.

Notes

NOTES TO INTRODUCTION

1. The period of the censuses, it must be remembered, spans the Civil War, in which more than 10 percent of the population was removed from the personal estates of the slaveholders to become potential propertyholders themselves.
2. W. Lloyd Warner, Marchia Meeker, and Kenneth Eells, *Social Class in America* (New York: Harper Torchbooks, 1960), pp. 140-41.
3. This table is described in chapter 6 below.
4. Reference is made to percentage changes in wealth per adult male, Kuznets's gross national product per worker, and Gallman's commodity output per worker. See Simon Kuznets, *Economic Growth and Structure* (New York: W. W. Norton, 1965), p. 305; and Robert Gallman, "Commodity Output, 1839-1899," in *Trends in the American Economy in the Nineteenth Century,* ed. William N. Parker, vol. 24, *Studies in Income and Wealth,* National Bureau of Economic Research (Princeton: Princeton University Press, 1960), pp. 16, 43. Wealth changes are computed from figures adjusted for slaves given in chapter 5.
5. Lee Soltow, "The Censuses of Wealth of Men in Australia in 1915 and in the United States in 1860 and 1870," *Australian Economic History Review* 12, no. 2 (1972), 125-41; "Economic Inequality in the United States in the Period from 1790 to 1860," *Journal of Economic History* 31, no. 4 (1971), 822-39.
6. Robert Gallman, "Trends in the Size Distribution of Wealth in the Nineteenth Century: Some Speculations," in *Six Papers on the Size Distribution of Wealth and Income,* ed. Lee Soltow, vol. 33, *Studies in Income and Wealth,* National Bureau of Economic Research (New York: Columbia University Press, 1969).

NOTES TO CHAPTER 1

1. B. R. Mitchell, *Abstract of British Historical Statistics* (Cambridge, England: Cambridge University Press, 1962), p. 38.
2. Each age-specific population is divided by an index in making an allowance for estimated deaths. This index is determined from published death rates by assuming that the proportion living in a year was 1 minus the death rate. These probabilities are multiplied to determine the index of living from age 20 to a given age. The equation shown by the straight line (DD for ages 20-69) in chart 1.1 is $N = 186,000 (1.029)^{20\text{-age}}$, where N is the death-inflated population of 1850 native born. (The line was plotted as .1N.)
3. U.S. Bureau of the Census, *Historical Statistics of the United States, Colonial Times to 1957* [Washington, D.C.: Government Printing Office (hereafter

GPO), 1960], series A 71-85, 45-47. Certain age–class interpolations have been made for 1800, 1810, and 1820. If native born increased 3 percent a year from 1840 to 1850, foreign born increased 10 percent a year.

4. Ibid., series D37 and D38.

5. Raymond W. Goldsmith, "The Growth of Reproducible Wealth of the United States of America from 1805 to 1950," in *Income and Wealth of the United States: Trends and Structure,* International Association for Research in Income and Wealth, Income and Wealth Series II (Cambridge, England: Bowes and Bowes, 1952), p. 269; Simon Kuznets, *Economic Growth and Structure* (New York: W. W. Norton, 1965), p. 305.

NOTES TO CHAPTER 2

1. U.S. Bureau of the Census, *Historical Statistics of the United States, Colonial Times to 1957* (Washington, D.C.: GPO, 1960), p. 206.

2. A sample of 5,386 adult males was drawn from the Ontario microfilm of the 1871 Census of Canada, and data were collated with manuscript schedules in the National Archives of Canada. This study will be called the Ontario sample. I have written a preliminary paper entitled "Illiteracy and Economic Accumulation in Ontario in 1871."

3. Lee Soltow, *Patterns of Wealthholding in Wisconsin Since 1850* (Madison: University of Wisconsin Press, 1971), pp. 78-79, 94. There were foreign born in many farm counties who were not given any occupational classification. Perhaps these people were in staging areas, preparing for further movement westward.

4. A sample of size 980 was drawn from the microfilm rolls of tax assessments (including poll taxes) of all free adult males 21 and older in Kentucky in 1800. The number of men recorded in the rolls is in excellent accord with the number recorded in the Federal Census of Kentucky in 1800. I describe these data more fully later in the chapter.

5. Ontario sample.

6. Personal estate of less than $100 in value generally was not reported in 1870. The proportion holding estate of $1 or more in 1860 was .646. Very few people reported real estate of less than $100 in any of the years.

7. The proportion of free reporting $1 or more of wealth in 1870 could be estimated to be .61 since the proportion reporting $1 or more in 1860 was .66.

8. As will be seen later, the TEH of older people is, at best, .80. This suggests a $1 - TEH$ group of .20, provided there were no young and particularly no unattached young in cities. A Wisconsin sample showed that one-third of sons with no wealth, but living in the same household with fathers, had fathers with no wealth.

9. Dorothy S. Projector, *Survey of Changes in Family Finances,* Federal Reserve Technical Papers (Washington, D.C.: Federal Reserve Board, Nov. 1968), p. 6, with reference to data from 1880 to 1950.

10. U.S. Census Office, 8th Census, 1860, *Population of the United States in 1860* (Washington, D.C.: GPO, 1864), pp. xxii, xxiii, 656-80.
11. David A. Wells, later president of the American Social Science Association and Commissioner of Revenue, publicized a study of immigrants arriving in New York in 1855-56 which showed that *average* money holdings were $86 for each man, woman, and child [David A. Wells, *Our Burden and Strength* (New York: Loyal Publication Society, 1864), p. 3; and *Population of the United States in 1860*, p. xxiii].
12. Francis Bowen, 2nd ed. (Boston: Little, Brown, 1859), p. 113.
13. Ibid., pp. 122-23. Amasa Walker, lecturer in public economy at Amherst College, wrote in 1865-66, "Land here is so cheap, labor so much in demand, that no able-bodied man has any excuse for pauperism" [*The Science of Wealth: A Manual of Political Economy* (Boston: Little, Brown, 1866), p. 412].
14. *Historical Statistics of the United States, Colonial Times to 1957*, series B 163-175.
15. See Robert H. Bremner, *From the Depths, the Discovery of Poverty in the United States* (New York: New York University Press, 1956), pp. 80-81; J. C. Furnass, *The Americans, A Social History of the United States, 1587-1914* (New York: G. P. Putnam, 1969), pp. 314-51; and Sidney Lens, *Poverty: America's Enduring Paradox* (New York: Thomas Y. Crowell, 1969), pp. 105, 109. Amasa Walker stated in 1865-66 that paupers were .05 percent of the population in the United States in 1859, that England had 4.5 percent in 1859, Holland had 8.5 percent in 1855, and Belgium had 16 percent in 1846 [*Science of Wealth*, p. 412].
16. Bremner, *From the Depths*, p. 21.
17. The probability of not obtaining property in a year may be estimated from the 10-year figures as $(.793)^{1/10} = .978$. Its complement of .022 is the probability of obtaining property in one year. This roughly equals the annual increase in population, and the system seemingly leaves PH constant from year to year.
18. The correlation coefficient squared is .14 if data are fitted to the 10,393 cases and .90 if fitted to the weighted averages at each age from 20 to 99. The parabola implies that PH is zero at age 17 and is a maximum at age 60.
19. The squared quadratic mean of ages is substituted for the squared term in the formula.
20. There is evidence that individual and aggregate valuation in 1870 did not adequately reflect inflationary conditions.
21. The proportion of propertyholders who were farmers may be stated for detailed groups. An example of the strong similarity is:

	20-99	20-29	30-99
Native born, 1850	.668	.64	.68
Native born, 1860	.679	.65	.68

In 1850, .477 of the gainfully employed free males 15 and older were listed as being in agriculture. The figures for 1860 give a very imperfect guide of how many farm laborers there were in 1850. In 1860 part of those gainfully employed who were 10 and older could be classified as agricultural. Of them 24 percent were farm laborers and almost all the rest were farmers. These figures could, of course, be substantially different from those of our sample of 1850 males who were 20 and older. U.S. Census Office, 7th Census, 1850, *Compendium* (Washington, D.C.: GPO, 1854), p. lxvi. The superintendent notes that "other occupations" is nebulous and that laborers are not separated into farm laborers and nonfarm laborers.

22. Lee Soltow, "The Wealth, Income, and Social Class of Men in Large Northern Cities in the United States in 1860," in *Personal Distributions of Income and Wealth*, ed. James D. Smith, vol. 39, *Studies in Income and Wealth*, National Bureau of Economic Research (New York: National Bureau of Economic Research, 1975).

23. W. Lloyd Warner and Paul S. Hunt, *The Social Life of a Modern Community*, vol. 1, *Yankee City Series* (New Haven: Yale University Press, 1941), p. 88; W. Lloyd Warner and associates, *Democracy in Jonesville* (New York: Harper Torchbooks, 1964), pp. 24–25; W. Lloyd Warner, Marchia Meeker, and Kenneth Eels, *Social Class in America* (New York: Harper Torchbooks, 1960), pp. 14, 140–41, 165.

24. Edwin Leigh, "Illiteracy in the United States," *Annual Report of the Commissioner of Education, 1870*, table III, pp. 478–79. See also Charles Warren, "Illiteracy in the U.S. in 1870 and 1880," U.S. Bureau of Education, *Circulars of Information*, nos. 1–7, 1884.

25. There was wide dispersion in ages at the time of migration. For Swedish and Norwegian age data, see *Sveriges Officiela Statistik, Underdåniga Berättelse for året 1865* (Stockholm: 1867) and *Norges Offisielle Statistik, Folkemaendens Bevaegelse, 1866–1885*. See also U.S. Census Office, 7th Census, 1850, *Compendium*, p. 124.

26. *Historical Statistics, Colonial Times to 1957*, series A 51–58.

27. All the regression coefficients are significant at the 1 percent level.

28. A standardizing procedure was developed for determining how much more or less the probability of ownership was in a region in 1850 than would have been expected on the basis of the age, nativity, and occupation of people in that region. The following table presents the actual PH minus expected PH by region number.

Region	Difference				
1	+ .06	4	+ .01	7	+ .07
2	− .04	5	+ .04	8	− .07
3	− .05	6	+ .08	9	− .01

Regions 2–8 present a clear pattern. Region 2 (Mass., Conn., R.I.) had 4 fewer persons with property per 100 than might have been expected on the basis of the number of farmers, the number of foreign born, and the number of young that it had. Region 3 (N.Y., N.J.) contributed the least toward ownership, and region 6 (Ind., Ill., Mich.) contributed the greatest positive effect. The contribution rises from region 2 to 6 and then diminishes. If correction had been made for age and nativity but not for the proportion of farmers in the region, the net contributions would have been

more dramatic. In this case they would have ranged from −.10 in region 2 to +.15 in region 7.

The expected $PH = \Sigma_{ano} PH_{U.S., ano} \times N_{reg, ano}$, where $PH_{U.S., ano}$ is the matrix of 24 PH values for the United States for six age classes, two nativity classes, and two occupation classes in 1850. These values (in abbreviated form for the four higher age groups) are given in table 2.3. The $N_{reg, ano}$ are the corresponding population elements or weights whose sum is 1.

29. Soltow, *Patterns of Wealthholding*, pp. 6, 7, 10.
30. Walker, *Science of Wealth*, p. 104; see also Bowen, *Principles of Political Economy*, pp. 86-87.
31. There is one disadvantage in using birth classifications. The individual may have moved with his parents from the Northeast at a very young age and not have been faced with the issue of betterment. The number of years of residence would have given a better index but such information was not available in the Federal Census.
32. Bowen, *Principles of Political Economy*, pp. 99-100.
33. G. P. Watkins, "The Growth of Large Fortunes," *Publications of the American Economic Association*, 3rd series, vol. 8 (1907); and James Bryce, *The American Commonwealth*, 2 vols. (New York: Macmillan, 1895).
34. Carroll D. Wright, "Are the Rich Growing Richer and the Poor Poorer?" *Atlantic Monthly* 80 (1897), 300-09.
35. The figures would have shown a drop from .62 to .53 if we had worked with data for 1860 freemen.
36. A three-way cross-classification table encompassing six age classes, two nativity classes, and two occupation classes is used for $PH_{ano, 1870}$ and population weights $N_{ano, 1960}$ in obtaining $.58 = \Sigma_{ano} (PH_{ano} N_{ano}) / \Sigma_{ano} N_{ano}$.
37. The ownership proportion in a given year has the familiar parabola when classified by age. This is true for the available age-specific figures in 1890, 1930, and 1940. The parabola may be made a straight line if the proportion is plotted opposite the log of adult age. The resulting line, $Y = a + b \log(age - 18)$, has a slope b, that is constant for the many years of data. The values are (b of PH_{1850}, PH_{1860}, $PH_{1870 W}$, $PH_{1870 free}$, HOH_{1890}, HOH_{1930}, HOH_{1940}) = (.48, .47, .52, .48, .52, .50, .48). See U.S. Census, 1890, *Farms and Homes: Proprietorship and Indebtedness*, tables 81 and 161; *Population and Housing, Families, General Characteristics*, 1940, p. 32 for owners.
38. Simon Kuznets found an annual rate of growth in worker income in the United States from 1860 to 1960 of .0141 [*Economic Growth and Structure* (New York: W. W. Norton, 1965), p. 305]. Raymond W. Goldsmith's estimates of growth of reproducible tangible wealth yield annual rates per head of 2.5 percent from 1850 to 1900 and 1.3 percent from 1900 to 1950 ["The Growth of Reproducible Wealth of the United States of America from 1805 to 1950," in *Income and Wealth of the United States: Trends and Structure*, International Association for Research in

Income and Wealth, Income and Wealth Series II (Cambridge, England: Bowes and Bowes, 1952), p. 269].

39. See Merle Curti, *The Growth of American Thought,* 2nd ed. (New York: Harper & Row, 1951), pp. 299, 300; Bowen, *Principles of Political Economy,* pp. 89, 100, 112; Robert P. Sharkey, *Money, Class and Party* (Baltimore: Johns Hopkins Press, 1959), p. 213; Richard C. Wade, *The Urban Frontier, The Rise of Western Cities, 1790-1830* (Cambridge: Harvard University Press, 1959), pp. 109, 110; Joseph Dorfman, *The Economic Mind in American Civilization,* vol. 2 (New York: Viking, 1946-1959), pp. 638-41; and Langston Byllesby, *Observations on the Sources and Effects of Unequal Wealth* (New York: Lewis J. Nichols, 1826; reprint, New York: Russell and Russell, 1961), p. 22.

40. The sample was drawn from the tax assessment microfilm rolls.

41. Lee Soltow, "Economic Inequality in the United States in the Period from 1790 to 1860," *Journal of Economic History* 31, no. 4 (1971): 829-30, 834.

42. Ibid., p. 833. The five areas in 1800 were Md., N.C., S.C., Del., and D.C. Appendix table A3 gives proportions holding personal estates of $100 or more.

NOTES TO CHAPTER 3

1. Francis Bowen, *The Principles of Political Economy,* 2nd ed. (Boston: Little, Brown, 1859), p. 122.

2. Herman Melville, "Poor Man's Pudding and Rich Man's Crumbs," *Harper's Magazine* 9 (June 1854): 98.

3. I use the consumer price index throughout this book as the deflator. See U.S. Department of Labor, *Handbook of Labor Statistics, 1971* (Washington, D.C.: GPO, 1971), p. 253.

4. This calculation is based on average wealth per family of $20,982 in 1962-63 as determined by Dorothy Projector and Gertrude S. Weiss, *Survey of Financial Characteristics of Consumers,* Federal Reserve Technical Papers (Washington, D.C.: Federal Reserve Board, 1966), pp. 110, 148. The real estate portion stems from an estimate of John Kendrick that the value of structures and land was two-thirds the value of national wealth in 1967. See U.S. Bureau of the Census, *Statistical Abstract of the United States: 1969* (Washington, D.C.: GPO, 1969), p. 334.

5. Projector and Weiss, *Financial Characteristics,* p. 151.

6. Income in this ratio is income product per worker. See Simon Kuznets, *Economic Growth and Structure* (New York: W. W. Norton, 1965), p. 305.

7. An estimate of $1,223 for total estate adjusted for slaves in 1850 will be presented later in the chapter. The wealth/income ratio would then be 3/1.

8. Amasa Walker, *The Science of Wealth: A Manual of Political Economy* (Boston: Little, Brown, 1866), p. 62.

9. Simon Kuznets, *Modern Economic Growth* (New Haven: Yale University Press, 1966), p. 237. In this table Kuznets gives a capital/output ratio of 3.5 to 1 for the United States in 1850.

10. Ibid., p. 168, table 4.2.

11. The denominator of TE of free in 1860 is increased to include adult male slaves $(\overline{TE}_{all, 1860})$, and the numerator is reduced by the estimate of slave value in obtaining $\overline{TE}_{slave\ adj,\ 1860}$. The 1850 estimate is $\overline{TE}_{slave\ adj,\ 1850}$ = $\overline{RE}_{all,\ 1850} \times \overline{TE}_{slave\ adj,\ 1860}/\overline{RE}_{all,\ 1860}$.

12. Kuznets, *Economic Growth and Structure*, p. 305; Robert Gallman, "Commodity Output, 1839-1899," in *Trends in the American Economy in the Nineteenth Century*, ed. William N. Parker, vol. 24, *Studies in Income and Wealth*, National Bureau of Economic Research (Princeton: Princeton University Press, 1960), pp. 16, 43.

13. Raymond W. Goldsmith, "The Growth of Reproducible Wealth of the United States of America from 1805 to 1950," in *Income and Wealth of the United States: Trends and Structure*, International Association for Research in Income and Wealth, Income and Wealth Series II (Cambridge, England: Bowes and Bowes, 1952), pp. 247, 306, 315.

14. Lee Soltow, *Patterns of Wealthholding in Wisconsin Since 1850* (Madison: University of Wisconsin Press, 1971), p. 26.

15. Bowen, *Principles of Political Economy*, pp. 99-100.

16. *Worth and Wealth, a Collection of Maxims, Morals, and Miscellanies for Merchants and Men of Business* (New York), pp. 62-64.

17. Estates of deceased, classified by age, are available in many places for previous centuries. There are a few local records with the ages and taxes of individuals recorded.

18. The squared correlation coefficient, R^2, is .02, and the standard error of the regression coefficient, SE_b, is $3.51.

19. Wealth is a function of age and time, $W = f(age, time) = f(a, t)$ and age is a function of time, $a = g(t)$; $\frac{dW}{dt} = \frac{\partial W}{\partial a}\frac{da}{dt} + \frac{\partial W}{\partial t}$. In the case of the individual, $\frac{da}{dt} = 1$, so our two effects are additive. For $W = b(adult\ age)e^{rt}$, $\frac{dW}{dt} / W = 1/(adult\ age) + r = AGR = GGR$.

20. Bowen, *Principles of Political Economy*, p. 110.

21. Alexis de Tocqueville, *Democracy in America*, abridged by Richard D. Heffner (New York: New American Library, Mentor Books, 1956), p. 159.

22. The difference in the regression coefficients for occupation is statistically significant at the 5 percent level. The dollar standard errors (S_b), sample size (n), and coefficient of determination (R^2) for the three equations appear in the accompanying table.

	age	nA	FB	So	n	R^2
1870 all	6	171	199	181	9,823	.05
1870 white	6	190	213	214	8,727	.05
1860 free	6	192	220	211	13,696	.03

23. The estimate of the Northwest advantage depends on the extent of standardization. This relationship is illustrated by the following equations
fitted to the wealth of individuals in the North in 1870:

$$TE = + \$2,895 - \$25 \text{ NW}$$
$$TE = - 2,334 + 133 \text{ age} + 163 \text{ NW}$$
$$TE = - 1,802 + 130 \text{ age} - 606 \text{ nA} + 21 \text{ NW}$$
$$TE = - 1,664 + 132 \text{ age} - 235 \text{ nA} - 1,664 \text{ FB} + 126 \text{ NW}$$

24. I conducted an investigation into differences between wealth in the Southwest, including Kentucky and Tennessee, and the Southeast. Average wealth
in the Southwest was about 5–10 percent greater among whites in 1860 and
1870. The average wealth was a third larger in the Southwest than in the
Southeast in 1870 if one considers both whites and nonwhites.

25. Lee Soltow, "The Economic Heritage of an Iowa County," forthcoming in
Annals of Iowa, A Historical Quarterly, August 1975.

26. "The Growth of Reproducible Wealth of the United States of America
from 1805 to 1950," in *Income and Wealth of the United States: Trends
and Structure,* International Association for Research in Income and Wealth,
Income and Wealth Series II (Cambridge, England: Bowes and Bowes, 1952),
p. 269.

27. *Statistical Abstract of the United States: 1969,* p. 334.

28. U.S. Bureau of the Census, *Historical Statistics of the United States, 1789-
1945* (Washington, D.C.: GPO, 1949), series A2.

29. Ibid., pp. 1, 9, table 1, series A1, A2; U.S. Bureau of the Census, *Historical
Statistics of the United States, Colonial Times to 1957* (Washington, D.C.:
GPO, 1960), p. 152, series F222; David Wells, *Our Burden and Our Strength*
(London: Loyal Publication Society, 1864), p. 8. A semilogarithmic trend
was fitted to the 30 estimates.

30. An example is the published average of $2,257 for cash value in 1850 and
spin-sample real estate of $2,281 for farmers (having $1 or more of real
estate) in 1850.

31. The apparent growth rate is the same in each year if the 1962-63 mean wealth
is adjusted to the mean age in 1870. The specific least-squares equations for
1870 and 1962-63 are $TE = \$110(\text{age} - 17.3)$ and $W = \$672(\text{age} - 16.6)$ for
the data of table 3.6. The AGR are $110/2,399 = .0468$ and $672/14,900 =
.0452$.

32. Each wealth mean for the five age classes in 1962-63 has been multiplied by
the corresponding population of adult males in 1870 in that age class. The
aggregate of these five products has been divided by the total adult population of 1870 to obtain the mean of $14,900.

33. Evidence has been presented in chart 2.1 that the wealth–age gradient is approximately linear, with the form $W = b(\text{age} - K)$. Least-squares equations
fitted to the real estate data for each census year give values of K between
15.7 and 18.0 years and $AGR_W = b/\overline{W}$ between .046 and .053. Total estate
gradients in 1860 and 1870 yield similar results with rates of .046-.049.

34. Death rates employed were those for Massachusetts in 1865 and England
in 1851, 1861, and 1871.

35. Adult age is age − K, where K is about 18.
36. The apparent growth rate of wealth in 1860 leads to a difference of .046 − .030 = .016. The aging of the population in subsequent decades might have reduced the difference to .040 − .025, or .035 − .020.
37. Walker, *Science of Wealth,* p. 62.
38. Lee Soltow, "The Growth of Wealth in Ohio, 1800-1969," in *Essays in Nineteenth Century Economic History—The Old Northwest,* ed. David Klingaman and Richard Vedder (Athens: Ohio University Press, 1975).
39. Kuznets, *Economic Growth and Structure,* p. 305.
40. Projector and Weiss, *Financial Characteristics,* pp. 110, 148. The ratio is 2.9 if Kuznets's income is used. John Kendrick has estimated the ratio of total wealth (including public assets) to net national product to have dropped from 5.6 in 1900 to 3.9 in 1967. See *Statistical Abstract of the United States: 1969,* p. 334. Kuznets lists a capital/output ratio of 3.5 in 1850 and 2.7 in 1950 in *Modern Economic Growth,* p. 76.
41. *Modern Economic Growth,* p. 237.
42. A presentation in terms of the apparent growth rate AGR_W at 5 percent or less is technically more appealing since income of others will be rising at the same time both before and after retirement. See Lee Soltow, "Retirement and Productivity," *Review of Economics and Statistics* 43, no. 1 (1961): 90-92.
43. The $\overline{TE}_{slave\ adj,\ 1860}$ value of $1,853 (see table 3.2) is multiplied by the consumer price index of 3.4 and compared to the wealth average in 1962-63.

NOTES TO CHAPTER 4

1. Lee Soltow, "Long-Run Changes in British Income Inequality" *Economic History Review* 21, no. 1 (1968): 28.
2. One extension of the Federal Reserve data supplemented by estimates of the Bureau of Internal Revenue gives the data of the accompanying table.

N_X	A_X, 1962-63	A_X, 1850
.0001	.04	.03
.001	.10	.12

Further details are given in table 4.5.
3. Alexis de Tocqueville, *Democracy in America,* abridged by Richard D. Heffner (New York: New American Library, Mentor Books, 1956), p. 161.
4. See Lee Soltow, "Shares of Lower Income Groups in Income," *Review of Economics and Statistics* 47, no. 4 (1965): 429-33.
5. It would have been an unsurmountable task to collate the wealth declaration of the individual with the census of slaves.
6. The 99th percentile (N_X = .01) in 1860 was $24,500 in the North and $57,500 in the South.
7. The real estate proportion of 2/3 held at all wealth levels and one wonders

if it did not also hold true in 1790. It would have bearing on the thesis of the Beards concerning the interest of the wealthy in particular monetary policies of government at the time of the Constitution's adoption.

8. The census lists 69 families living in Washington City of the District of Columbia with 5 or more slaves each. The corresponding figure for Baltimore City is 56.

9. In 1870 domestic servants constituted 14 percent of the stated occupations of persons in New York City, 11 percent in Cincinnati, and 20 percent in New Orleans.

10. A Gini coefficient of .89 seemed to be an almost universal figure for urban societies. Eight of ten major urban counties in the North in 1860 had coefficients between .89 and .91.

11. If set U is partitioned into two subsets A and B, and the greatest wealth value of A is less than or equal to the lowest of B, then $N_U^2 \bar{X}_U G_U = N_A^2 \bar{X}_A G_A + N_B^2 \bar{X}_B G_B + N_A N_B (\bar{X}_B - \bar{X}_A)$. An extreme case would be where $N_A = .2$, $N_B = .8$, $\bar{X}_A = 0$, $\bar{X}_B = 1$, and $G_A = 0$. In this case, $G_U = .8 G_B + .2$; if $G_A = .8$, G_U is only increased to .84.

12. Thomas F. Pettigrew, "Symposium of Jenck's Inequality," *American Journal of Sociology* 79 (May 1973): 1528.

13. It is true that equations for the North do have larger coefficients associated with occupation. Here we have

$$1870: \ G_{TE} = .859 - .0051 \ \text{age} + .152 \ nA + .0002 \ FB,$$
$$1860: \ G_{TE} = .866 - .0047 \ \text{age} + .137 \ nA - .0009 \ FB.$$

14. Carroll D. Wright, "Are the Rich Growing Richer and the Poor Poorer?" *The Atlantic Monthly* 80 (1897), 300-09.

15. "The Growth of Large Fortunes," *Publications of the American Economic Association,* 3rd series, vol. 8.

16. C. A. Beard and M. R. Beard, *The Rise of American Civilization,* vol. 2, The Industrial Era (New York: Macmillan, 1927), pp. 383-84.

17. Matthew Josephson, *The Robber Barons* (New York: Harcourt, Brace, 1934); see also Gustavus Myers, *History of the Great American Fortunes,* 3 vols. (Chicago: C. H. Kerr, 1911); and Ferdinand Lundberg, *America's 60 Families* (New York: Vanguard Press, 1937).

18. *Rise of American Civilization,* pp. 383-84.

19. *The Share of Top Wealth-Holders in National Wealth* (Princeton: Princeton University Press, 1962), p. 256. A smaller number is given if an adjustment is made for insurance.

20. U.S. Treasury Department, Internal Revenue Service, *Personal Wealth Estimated from Estate Tax Returns,* supplemental report of May 1967, pp. 20, 35. The number of male millionaires was 31,000-37,000.

21. Lee Soltow, "Evidence on Income Inequality in the United States, 1866-1965," *Journal of Economic History* 29, no. 2 (1969): 279-86.

22. These frequency tables are given in U.S. Treasury Department, *Statistics of Income,* various issues.

23. *Share of Top Wealth-Holders,* p. 25; also, "National Wealth: Distribution," in *International Encyclopedia of the Social Sciences,* vol. 11, ed. David L. Sills (New York: Macmillan, 1968), p. 62.

24. The median county in Wisconsin in 1860 had 30 percent of its men with
no wealth who were attached to families with wealth. If this proportion
holds for the United States in 1870, 13 percent of males could be sub-
sumed in families and the Gini coefficient would drop to .805.

25. Three assumptions were made in developing the distribution: (1) The
tenants have no wealth. (2) The encumbered have a distribution with a
relative dispersion equal to that of gross values but with a mean equivalent
to equity value. (3) The owners without encumberances have the same
relative dispersion as the encumbered but with ownership large enough
to give all houses an average equivalent to that of the known gross value
of the encumbered. George Holmes made somewhat the same assumptions
in "The Concentration of Wealth," *Political Science Quarterly* 8, no. 4
(1893): 589-600.

26. Indiana Department of Statistics, *Eighth Biennial Report for 1899 and
1900* (Indianapolis: Wm. B. Burford, 1900), pp. 459-553.

27. Lee Soltow, "Economic Inequality in the United States in the Period from
1790 to 1860," *Journal of Economic History* 31, no. 4 (1971): 828.

28. Massachusetts Bureau of Statistics of Labor, *Twenty-Fifth Annual Report,*
Public Document no. 15 (Boston: 1895), pp. 264-67. The Pareto curves
tested are those for males. An alternative presentation is given in G. P.
Watkins, "An Interpretation of Certain Statistical Evidence of Concen-
tration of Wealth," *Journal of the American Statistical Association* 11
(March 1908): 37.

29. *Observations on the Sources and Effects of Unequal Wealth* (New York:
Lewis J. Nichols, 1826; reprint New York: Russell and Russell, 1961),
p. 22. Joseph Dorfman has called the work the "first systematic American
treatise" in *The Economic Mind in American Civilization* (5 vols.), vol. 2
(New York: Viking, 1946-59), pp. 638-41.

30. The lognormal curve technically has a Pareto form that is a curved line.

31. The form $Z = \log$ (total estate + \$10) was used to obviate the influence
of very small values.

32. A picture of Kapteyn's analog machine for generating such a distribution
using marbles is given in J. Aitchison and J. A. C. Brown, *The Lognormal
Distribution, with Special Reference to Its Uses in Economics* (Cambridge,
England: Cambridge University Press, 1969), facing p. 23.

33. Further justification for use of the procedure in estimating saving and
consumption is given in Lee Soltow, "The Wealth, Income, and Social
Class of Men in Large Northern Cities in the United States in 1860," in
Personal Distributions of Income and Wealth, ed. James D. Smith, vol. 39,
Studies in Income and Wealth, National Bureau of Economic Research
(New York: National Bureau of Economic Research, 1975).

34. Lee Soltow, "Evidence on Income Inequality in the United States, 1866-
1965," *Journal of Economic History* 29, no. 2 (1969): 279-86.

35. Dorothy S. Projector, *Survey of Changes in Family Finances,* Federal
Reserve Technical Papers (Washington, D.C.: Federal Reserve Board, Nov.
1968), pp. 6, 214, 321, 52. Some consumption data for 1874-75 and
1889-91 give essentially the same idea. See U.S. Bureau of the Census,

Historical Statistics of the United States, Colonial Times to 1957 (Washington, D.C.: GPO, 1960), series G 315-16, 324-26.

36. Income distribution today is of this shape below the median.

37. *Modern Economic Growth* (New Haven: Yale University Press, 1966), p. 237.

38. Simon Kuznets, *Economic Growth and Structure* (New York: W. W. Norton, 1965), p. 305.

39. Lee Soltow, *Patterns of Wealthholding in Wisconsin Since 1850* (Madison: University of Wisconsin Press, 1971), p. 86, table 19. Board and room costs averaged about $20 a month in most states in 1870. See House Executive Documents 1-10, serial #1470, vol. 1, *Information for Immigrants,* Expenses of Living, pp. 224-30, 216-17.

40. I know of only one comprehensive consumption distribution for mid-century. It is the distribution of rooms among families in Scotland in 1861. The top 1.86 percent of families had 12 percent of the rooms and all families had at least one room. See Lee Soltow, "An Index of the Poor and Rich of Scotland, 1861-1961," *Scottish Journal of Political Economy* 18, no. 1 (1971): 49-67.

NOTES TO CHAPTER 5

1. Tocqueville did recognize that slaves made it possible for there to be rich landed proprietors in the South. Alexis de Tocqueville, *Democracy in America,* abridged by Richard D. Heffner (New York: New American Library, Mentor Books, 1956), p. 159.

2. Frederick Jackson Turner, "The Significance of the Frontier in American History," in *Frontier and Section,* ed. Ray Allen Billington (Englewood Cliffs, N.J.: Prentice-Hall, 1961), p. 39.

3. These numbers stem from using midpoints of 1,500 (a Pareto extrapolation), 600, 150, 60, 30, 13, and 5 for the above classes.

4. The projection is based on the least-squares equation $A = 42.0 \, N_A^{-.55}$, stemming from the first four points of table 5.1.

5. *The Science of Wealth: A Manual of Political Economy* (Boston: Little, Brown), p. 412.

6. See Bernard Bailyn, *The Ideological Origins of the American Revolution* (Cambridge: Harvard University Press, Belknap Press, 1967), p. 308.

7. Southern and western regions are excluded. Only six classes have been used in the computation of G for each year. They have lower class limits of 1,000, 500, 100, 50, 10, and 0 or 3 acres. Separate estimates of G in 1860 and 1870 of .40 and .42, respectively, can be obtained with more conservative midpoints. Improved land as a proportion of total land for all farms in the North was .514 in 1850, .577 in 1860, .611 in 1870, and .727 in 1880.

8. Just how much land inequality existed prior to 1850 is not known. The Kentucky sample for the year 1800 shows very great inequality of land ownership with 1 percent of men owning 50 percent of the state's land.

9. This is a computation from a frequency table of 21 classes, including those with assumed midpoints of 1,500, 750, 400, 250, 150, 85, 60, 45, 35, 25, 17, and 12. This gives a total of 3,900,000 slaves, as contrasted to the reported 3,953,742 slaves.

10. I computed the county average by dividing the published census aggregate of personal estate for the county by the number of freemen in the county. Values would be 7–8 percent less if wealth of women and children had been eliminated. The average for each slave class above is not weighted by population but rather is the sum of the county averages divided by the number of counties.

11. Real estate aggregates were used instead of personal estate aggregates in the 16 counties. Four of them were in this top slave class. In addition there is a peculiarity about Isaquena County, Mississippi, the county with the largest average number of slaves, 32 (determined from a special study of slaveholders in the county).

12. Two equations of interest developed from the 1860 spin sample for the United States are

$$PE = \$ \ 37 + \$ \ 45age + \$ \ \ 0nA - \$ \ \ 542FB + \$1,466So, \ and$$
$$TE = \ \ 684 + \ \ 110age - \ \ 428nA - \ \ 1,211FB + \ \ 1,749So.$$

The +$1,466 differential in the South (So = 1) would amount to $733 per slave if one were to attribute the effect solely to the fact that there were 2.0 slaves per adult male in the South. The differential for real estate would have been much larger than $283 if it were thought that this was the added land value farmed by slaves.

13. *Annual Cyclopaedia, 1869* (New York: D. Appleton, 1870), p. 637, gives a table for South Carolina that indicates pricing at about the same figures in 1860 and 1869. The accompanying table lists assessed value of livestock in its entirety.

	1869		*1860*	
	Number	*Value*	*Number*	*Value*
Horses	50,071	$3,925,580	81,125	—
Cattle	270,987	2,589,969	506,776	—
Mules and asses	39,257	3,611,671	56,456	—
Sheep and goats	164,421	198,664	233,509	—
Hogs	468,373	1,450,424	965,779	—
Total	993,109	11,776,308	1,843,645	$23,934,465

If the implicit prices of 1869 are applied to the number in 1860, a value of $19.7 million is obtained.

14. The mean number of slaves in 1850 and 1860 were 9.2 and 10.3 per slaveholder and 2.1 and 2.0 per free man. Corresponding Gini coefficients were .595 and .619 for slaveholders and .906 and .926 for free men.

15. From an article in *The New York Times,* Jan. 12, 1854, in *The Cotton Kingdom,* ed. Arthur Schlesinger (New York: Knopf, 1953), p. 558.

16. Lee Soltow, "Economic Inequality in the United States in the Period from

1790 to 1860," *Journal of Economic History* 31, no. 4 (1971): 825-26.
17. Ibid., pp. 828-29.
18. Lee Soltow, "A Century of Personal Wealth Accumulation" (from a paper read at the workshop in economic history, University of Chicago), in *The Economics of Black Americans,* ed. Harold G. Vatter and Thomas Palm, (New York: Harcourt, Brace, Jovanovich, 1972), pp. 30-34.

NOTES TO CHAPTER 6

1. The equation is $TE/\overline{TE} = .061(age - 21.6)$.
2. The apparent growth rate AGR was .044 in 1860 for total estate.
3. The Registrar General, *The Census of Scotland of 1861,* Edinburgh, p. xxx.
4. The sole equation employed in conjunction with the United States data was $TE = a + b\ age + c\ So_{res} + \Sigma d_i\ birth_i; i = 1, 2, 3, \ldots, 13; birth_i = 1$ if the person was born in the region and 0 if not; $So_{res} = 1$ if the person lived in the South and 0 if he did not. For the United States, age = 37.6 and $So_{res} = .279$. The equation value for the ith region was determined by letting age = 37.6, $So_{res} = 0$ for (1) and .279 for (2), $birth_i = 1$, and $birth_{i \neq i} = 0.0$. In the case of Ohio, $2,657 = -2,713 + 110.3(37.6) + 1,770(.279) + 727(1.0)$. The same general equation was fitted only to northern figures.
5. The Ontario sample of size 5,386 described in n. 2 of chapter 2.
6. The average age in (4) is one year more than that in (3). About $90-$100 should be subtracted from (4) values before making comparisons with (3).
7. There is statistical evidence from annual Ohio appraisals that average wealth rose much more rapidly during the settlement period from 1800 to 1850 than it did after the Civil War.
8. The coefficient for So_{res} is larger than that for So_{bir} in $TE_{U.S., 1860} = -2,151 + 110\ age + 32\ NE_{res} + 513NE_{bir} + 1,774So_{res} + 437So_{bir} - 895FB$. The addition of six cross-product terms for residence and birth leaves essentially the same values.
9. For various reasons, 37 counties had to be eliminated.
10. I obtained the average wealth for a county by dividing the aggregate by the number of free men. This yields, perhaps, an average 5-10 percent larger than if the wealth of women and children had been subtracted from the aggregate. The ratio is designated ($0/af) since nothing has been deducted in the numerator for the valuations of slaveholdings and only whites and free colored have been considered in the denominator. The values of G are computed assuming each man has the average of his county.
11. The Gini coefficient is the expected value of paired differences divided by two times the mean.
12. I took a small spin sample of women and children with wealth and found that their aggregate wealth was 7.8 percent of men's wealth. The number of women and children with wealth as a proportion of the number of adult males for the United States, the North, and South was, respectively, .059, .054, and .069.

13. Regression equations fitted to the 963 points were TE = $1,299 + $110 age, and TE = -$1,303 + $93 age - $1,440 FB. Spin-sample results were TE = -$1,424 + $92 age and TE = $1,015 + $90 age - $1,152 FB.

14. The northern equation for the variables is log TE = 3.00 + .238 log D, R^2 = .40, n = 963; TE = 1,000 $D^{.238}$ = 2,180$(1.01)^t$ if D = 26$(1.04)^t$.

15. The northern coefficient of determination is R^2 (log TE, log CV) = .50 in one case and R^2 (log CV; log D, log I) = .81 in the other.

16. Production function forms of interest are log TE = 2.4140 + .1130 log wage + .4033 log CV, R^2 = .53; and log TE = .8401 + .3427 log I + .0884 log mfg, R^2 = .65.

17. Recall that our county averages come from published aggregates that include wealth of women and children.

Index

Age: cohorts, 64; composition, 9-12; importance of, 9, 27, 69; and inequality, 48-49, 110; of nativity and occupation groups, 12-19; and propertyholder and total estate proportions, 27-33, 51, 58-59; and time, 30-31; and wealth, 69-74, 85. *See also* Frequency distributions; Gini coefficients of inequality; Income; Inequality; Multiple regression; Personal estate proportion; Poor men; Propertyholder proportion; Real estate; Saving; Total estate; Total estate proportion

Aitchison, J., 197n

Apparent growth rate (AGR): and general growth rate (GGR), 73, 85; a model, 73, 86-88; in population, 12-19; in wealth, 72-73, 193n19

Australian wealth, 6, 26

Bailyn, Bernard, 198n

Beard, Charles A. and Mary R., 111, 112 and n, 196n

Birth regions: and population, 184; wealth, 147-56; wealthholder proportions, 40, 44-46

Bowen, Francis, 26, 62, 69, 189n, 191n, 192n, 193n

Bremner, Robert H., 189n

Brown, J. A. C., 197n

Bryce, James, 46, 191n

Burchard, Horatio, 83 and n

Byllesby, Langston, 118 and n, 192n

Censuses: agricultural censuses, 131-32; home ownership, 49-51; published county data, 147, 156-66; *specific manuscript examples,* 2-3

Consumption: distribution, 121-22; equality of condition, 125; and rooms, 198n40

County analysis: bordering Mississippi River, 167-71; density of population, 165-66; economic characteristics, 158-59; improved acreage, 164-65; by longitude, 160-64; slaveholding, 137-40; wealth distribution, 156-60, 167-71

Curti, Merle, 192n

Death rates: and Civil War, 16-19; death-inflated population, 10-12, 15, 187n2; and hardship, 26; Massachusetts and England, 10

Dorfman, Joseph, 192n, 197n

Eels, Kenneth, 187n, 190n

Farmers: farm labor definition, 35 and n; and foreign born, 40; and home ownership, 50; and inequality, 108; population, 14-19; and property and total estate proportions, 32-36; rural-urban movement, 14-19, 91. *See also* Farms; Occupations; *Specific wealth subject*

Farms: acreage, 125-33; cash value, 83-84, 159, 166; farm and home census, 116-17; improved acreage, 159, 164-65; land availability, 131. *See also* County analysis

Federal Reserve Study, 51, 85, 88 and n, 94, 115, 183. *See also* Projector, Dorothy S.

Foreign born: handicaps, 22, 36-37, 39; inequality, 109; mean wealth, 76-79, 171-72; population, 12-13; wealthholder proportions, 36-40. *See also* Birth regions; *Specific wealth subject*

Frequency distributions: of acreage, 126, 127, 164; of age, 10, 11, 18, 58-59, 85; by color, 145; by density,